Fantastic FABRIC FOLDING

INNOVATIVE QUILTING PROJECTS

REBECCA WAT

C&T PUBLISHING

Editor: Joyce Engels Lytle

Technical Editor: Lynn Koolish

Design Director: Kathy Lee

Book Design: Christina Jarumay

Cover Design: Christina Jarumay

Illustrators: Jay Richards, Norman Remer

Cover: detail of *Springtime Impression* II

Back cover: *Springtime Impression* I

Photography: Sharon Risedorph

Library of Congress Cataloging-in-Publication Data

Wat, Rebecca
   Fantastic fabric folding : innovative quilting projects /
Rebecca Wat.
   p. cm.
 Includes bibliographical references (p.   ) and index.
 ISBN 1-57120-085-1 (paper trade)
 1. Quilting Patterns. 2. Origami. I. Title.
 TT835.W375 2000
 746.46--dc21
                              99-06610
                              CIP

Published by C&T Publishing, Inc.
P.O. Box 1456
Lafayette, California 94549

Printed in China
10

Dedication

To my parents, Hon-Yin and Wing-Yee, who never cease to believe in me.

Acknowledgments

I would like to thank all the nice ladies I came to know at my local quilt shop, the Laurel Leaf in San Carlos, California for their encouragement and help. They are Julie Murphy, Gwen Herrick, Jan Freeman, Virginia Dunlap, Dorothy Paneri, Lesley Johnson, and Gunvor Torre. I am particularly thankful to Julie, owner of the Laurel Leaf, for machine quilting *What's the Name of That Flower?*, *Star Within Star*, and *Starry, Starry Night*; Virginia for hand quilting *Three Topiaries* and *My Flower Garden*; Gwen for teaching me the basics of quilting; and Jan for introducing me to the Peninsula Quilters.

Thanks to Benartex, Inc. for providing beautiful fabrics shown in all the Folding Instructions in this book. Thanks to my editorial teammates at C&T Publishing, Joyce Lytle, Lynn Koolish, Diane Pedersen, Kathy Lee, and Christina Jarumay, for their wonderful ideas and input, and their relentless striving for perfection.

Moreover, I am grateful to Justina Chau, Cara Choy, Lily Tam, and Betty Wu for their friendship, encouragement, and moral support. I am also indebted to my husband, Watson, who is ever supportive to all my new ideas and was even willing to give up his computer for me to write the manuscript. Most of all, thanks to the Lord for giving me the courage to create *Fantastic Fabric Folding*.

Table of Contents

Introduction

$\mathcal{I}$t has been more than twenty-five years since I first fell in love with origami, the art of paper folding. Through the years, origami has given me solutions for problems from gift-wrapping to home decorating, and even helped me understand geometry. One day, driven by my own curiosity, I tried folding fabric instead of paper. I folded a rose, a pinwheel, and a star; then I either pieced the blocks together or stitched them onto other pieces of fabric. Over time, I created more than twenty one-of-a-kind projects.

In this book, I share with you all my techniques and designs. Each chapter is dedicated to the introduction of a single fabric origami design and a few related projects. The last chapter provides some basic construction techniques, which beginning quilters will find particularly useful. Among the twenty-two projects presented, some are new versions of popular traditional patterns, while others are absolutely unexpected and original in their form and style. In some cases, I have gone beyond the scope of quilting to demonstrate the versatility of these origami designs. In fact, these designs are so versatile that they can be applied to areas such as home decorating, gift-wrapping, and fashion design. Applying the designs to the making of wedding gowns was a suggestion from a gentleman, formerly in the textile industry, whom I met in a quilt shop.

How to Use This Book

Before beginning any particular project, I encourage you first to try some, if not all, of the origami blocks. Unlike many other existing three-dimensional designs, most of the origami blocks in this book are made of a single piece of fabric and are consequently quicker and easier to make. You just need to follow the folding instructions in each chapter. Practice with scrap fabric or paper to become familiar with the folding techniques and to give you a feel of the time and level of skill it takes for each project. Here are a few suggestions to follow while using this book:

Working on a Project

◆ Learn the required folding techniques first.

◆ Cut fabric to the exact size and shape.

◆ Follow the folding instructions closely and fold accurately.

◆ Finger-press means pressing firmly with your thumbnail.

◆ Iron-press refers to pressing with a steam iron with only up and down motions. You will need to iron-press seam allowances and set the folds.

◆ You may wish to use pins to help fold or sew the folded blocks together more accurately.

◆ Sew with a 1/4" seam allowance unless otherwise noted.

◆ Your skills and speed will improve tremendously as you practice the folds.

Choosing Fabrics

◆ Estimated yardage for projects is based on 40"-wide fabric.

◆ Experiment with fabrics of different colors, patterns, and textures.

◆ Choose fabrics that hold creases well. Cotton is the easiest to work with since it tends to hold creases better.

◆ Silk or silky fabrics usually need to be pressed with a press-cloth.

◆ Fabrics that are not pre-washed are easier to work with since they have more body.

◆ Wash these three-dimensional quilts exactly as you would wash any other quilt. If you plan to machine wash frequently, or do not want to press the folds again after washing, tack down the folds, especially the center of the folded designs.

Above all I hope you will find reading this book an enjoyable and inspiring experience. After becoming familiar with the fabric-folding techniques introduced here, you may even want to create new origami designs of your own. So have fun folding and sewing, and let your wings of creativity take flight.

Stars

"*T*winkle, twinkle little star, how I wonder what you are…" A first glance at this three-dimensional star design may make you wonder what it is, what it takes to create something like this. Made from a single square piece of fabric, this design has the cool, clean-cut look of a star with an interesting interlocking feature in the center. The design is totally symmetrical and can be used like any other square of fabric in a quilt pattern.

Step A

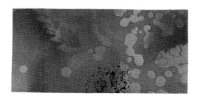

1. With the fabric wrong-side up, fold the square in half horizontally. Finger-press to make a crease along the fold line ($1/2$ crease line).

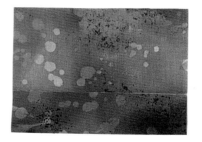

2. Open the fabric (wrong-side up). Bring the bottom raw edge up to align with the finger-pressed crease ($1/2$ crease line). Fold and finger-press ($1/4$ crease line).

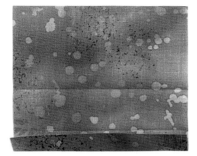

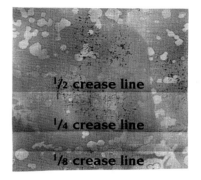

3. Open the fabric (wrong-side up). Bring the bottom raw edge up to align with the finger-pressed crease ($1/4$ crease line). Fold and finger-press ($1/8$ crease line).

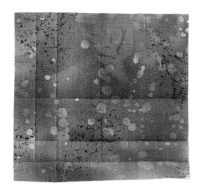

4. Rotate the fabric clockwise 90°, fold in half and finger-press to make $1/2$ crease line. Repeat Steps 2 and 3.

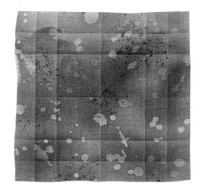

5. Repeat Step 4 on the remaining two sides of the fabric.

Step B

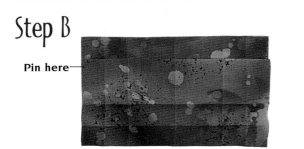

Pin here

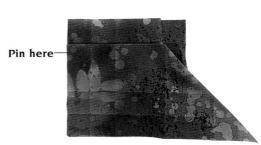

Pin here

6. With the fabric right-side up, bring the horizontal ½ crease line up to the ⅛ crease line. Finger-press. You may find it helpful to pin the fold on the edge of the left side, as you make all four of these folds.

7. Rotate the fabric clockwise 90°. Bring what remains of the horizontal ½ crease line up to the ⅛ crease line pulling the lower corner out to look like the photo above.

Pin here

8. Rotate the fabric clockwise 90°. Bring what remains of the horizontal ½ crease line up to the ⅛ crease line. Repeat for the last side.

9. Adjust the center to form a diamond shape, and iron-press to set the shape, removing any pins if you have used them.

Step C

Note: When making your quilt, complete Step C after the blocks are pieced together.

10. Bring the bottom corner of the center diamond up to the horizontal ½ crease line and finger-press.

11. Rotate the fabric counter clockwise 90°. Repeat Step 10 for the second corner.

12. Repeat Step 11 for the third corner.

13. Repeat Step 11 for the fourth corner. Iron-press to set the star shape.

Starry, Starry Night

Starry, Starry Night, 58" x 58", Rebecca Wat, quilted by Julie Murphy

Cutting and piecing squares together is one of the easiest ways to create quilt tops. *Starry, Starry Night* is primarily the result of this technique, except there is an extra step of folding and pressing the folded squares before they are pieced together. The use of three-dimensional stars makes the quilt look sophisticated and interesting while the contrasting background color creates added depth. The eight solid squares are important in that they create a focal point for the viewer.

Materials

Folded Stars:
>   Purple: 1 yard
>   Copper and Yellow: $3/4$ yard each
>   Aqua and Pink: $2/3$ yard each
>   Light Blue: $1/2$ yard
>   Multi-color: $1/2$ yard

Background (shown as gray): $1 1/2$ yards

Background, Borders and Binding (shown as black):
> $1 3/4$ yards

Contrasting Border: $1/4$ yard

Backing: $3 1/2$ yards

Batting: 62" x 62"

Cutting

Folded Stars: (Total of 117 squares)

◆ From purple, cut five 6"-wide strips, then cut strips into 6" squares. You will need 28 squares.

◆ From copper and yellow, cut four 6"-wide strips each, then cut strips into 6" squares. You will need 21 squares of each color.

◆ From aqua and pink, cut three 6"-wide strips each, then cut strips into 6" squares. You will need 15 squares of each color.

◆ From light blue, cut two 6"-wide strips, then cut strips into 6" squares. You will need 9 squares for the center.

◆ From multi-color, cut two 6"-wide strips, then cut strips into 6" squares. You will need 8 squares.

Background:

◆ Cut ten $3 3/4$"-wide strips, and then cut strips into $3 3/4$" squares. You will need 96 squares. (See cutting instructions below for the 8 black squares.)

◆ Cut two $3 1/8$" squares, and then cut both diagonally for 4 corner triangles.

◆ Cut ten $5 7/8$" squares, and then cut each diagonally twice for 40 setting triangles.

Borders and Binding: Refer to page 85 for help cutting correct lengths, if needed.

◆ Inner Black Border: Cut four $1 1/2$"-wide strips lengthwise.

◆ Outer Black Border: Cut four $2 1/2$"-wide strips lengthwise.

◆ Binding: Cut four $3 1/4$"-wide strips lengthwise from black border fabric. To make binding refer to pages 87-88.

◆ Background Squares (black): Cut one $3 3/4$"-wide strip from the remaining border fabric (black), then cut strip into $3 3/4$" squares. You will need 8 squares.

◆ Contrasting Border: Cut six 1"-wide strips crosswise (You will need to piece strips together end-to-end, then cut to the required lengths for your quilt.)

Folding

Fold and finger-press each 6" square following the steps shown in the Folding Instructions, pages 9-10. The folded squares should measure $3 3/4$". You should skip Step C until the whole quilt top is pieced.

Construction

1. Lay all the pieces onto a flat surface or a design board as shown. Using a $1/4$" seam allowance, sew blocks together in diagonal rows. Press (up and down motion) the seam allowances of each row in an alternate direction. (The alternately pressed seam allowances of the blocks should make matching the seams easier.)

Sewing blocks together in diagonal rows

2. Sew the rows together matching seams. Press the seam allowances in one direction.

3. Attach the side inner borders first, then the top and bottom inner borders. Press seams toward border. Repeat for the contrasting border and the outer border.

4. Refer to pages 86-88 for general quilting and finishing instructions.

Attaching borders

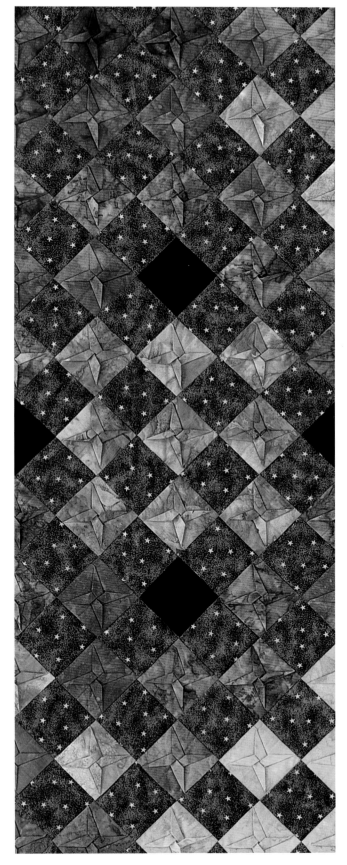

Star Within Star

Star Within Star, 50" x 50", Rebecca Wat, quilted by Julie Murphy

The Sawtooth Star pattern was adapted for *Star Within Star*. Using the folding techniques introduced in this chapter, place a three-dimensional star in each Sawtooth Star block. This gives a new look to the traditional pattern.

Materials

Stars:
    Fabric A: 1$\frac{1}{4}$ yards
    Fabric C: 1$\frac{1}{4}$ yards
Star Background:
    Fabric B: 1 yard
    Fabric D: $\frac{3}{4}$ yard
Inner Border: $\frac{1}{4}$ yard
Outer Border and Binding: 1$\frac{1}{2}$ yards
Backing: 3 yards
Batting: 54" x 54"

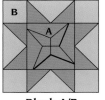 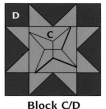

Block A/B   **Block C/D**

Cutting

Make a record of your fabric A, B, C, and D.

Folded Star Centers:
◆ From fabric A, cut three 7$\frac{1}{4}$"-wide strips, then cut strips into 7$\frac{1}{4}$" squares. You will need 13 squares.
◆ From fabric C, cut three 7$\frac{1}{4}$"-wide strips, then cut strips into 7$\frac{1}{4}$" squares. You will need 12 squares.

Star Points:
◆ From fabric A, cut seven 2$\frac{1}{2}$"-wide strips, then cut strips into 2$\frac{1}{2}$" squares. You will need 104 squares.
◆ From fabric C, cut six 2$\frac{1}{2}$"-wide strips, then cut strips into 2$\frac{1}{2}$" squares. You will need 96 squares.

Star Background:
◆ From fabric B, cut ten 2$\frac{1}{2}$"-wide strips, then cut strips into 2$\frac{1}{2}$" x 4$\frac{1}{2}$" rectangles and 2$\frac{1}{2}$" squares. You will need 52 rectangles and 52 squares.
◆ From fabric D, cut nine 2$\frac{1}{2}$"-wide strips, then cut strips into 2$\frac{1}{2}$" x 4$\frac{1}{2}$" rectangles and 2$\frac{1}{2}$" squares. You will need 48 rectangles and 48 squares.

Borders and Binding: Refer to page 85 for help cutting correct lengths, if needed.
◆ Inner Border: Cut five 1$\frac{1}{4}$"-wide strips crosswise (You will need to piece strips together end-to-end, then cut to the required length for your quilt.)
◆ Outer Border: Cut four 4$\frac{1}{2}$"-wide strips lengthwise.

◆ Binding: Cut four 3$\frac{1}{4}$" strips lengthwise from the remaining outer border fabric. To make binding refer to pages 87-88.

Folding

Fold and finger-press each 7$\frac{1}{4}$" square following steps shown in the Folding Instructions, pages 9-10. The folded squares should measure 4$\frac{1}{2}$". You may skip Step C and complete this last step after the quilt top is pieced together.

Construction

1. Fold each of the one hundred four 2$\frac{1}{2}$" squares (Fabric A) diagonally to form a crease line, or draw a line with a marking tool. This line is the stitching line for piecing the 2$\frac{1}{2}$" squares onto the 2$\frac{1}{2}$" x 4$\frac{1}{2}$" rectangles (Fabric B) to make the star points.

2. Fold each of the ninety-six 2$\frac{1}{2}$" squares (Fabric C) diagonally to form a crease line, or draw a line with a marking tool. This line is the stitching line for piecing the 2$\frac{1}{2}$" squares onto the 2$\frac{1}{2}$" x 4$\frac{1}{2}$" rectangles (Fabric D) to make the star points.

3. Make star points as shown.

Sew a 2$\frac{1}{2}$" square onto a 2$\frac{1}{2}$" x 4$\frac{1}{2}$" rectangle.

Trim off excess.
Press open.

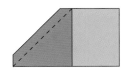

Sew a 2$\frac{1}{2}$" square onto the other corner of the 2$\frac{1}{2}$" x 4$\frac{1}{2}$" rectangle.
Trim off excess.

Press open.

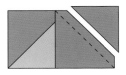

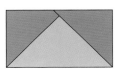

4. With a ¹/₄" seam allowance, sew all the pieces together as shown to form 25 blocks. Press.

Block construction

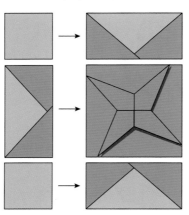

Step 1

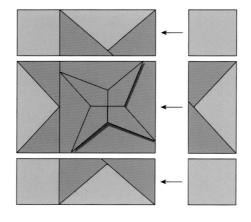

Step 2

5. Lay the blocks onto a flat surface or design board. Sew the blocks together creating five rows. Press seam allowances of each row in an alternate direction. (The alternately pressed seam allowances of the blocks should make matching the seams easier.) Then join the rows together, matching seams. Press seams in one direction.

6. Attach the side inner borders first, then the top and bottom inner borders. Press seams toward the border. Repeat for the outer border.

7. Refer to pages 86-88 for general quilting and finishing instructions.

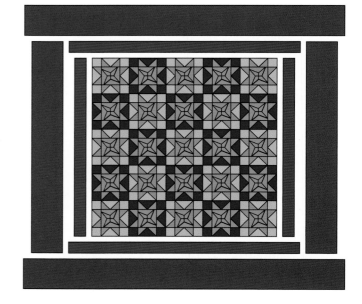

Attaching borders

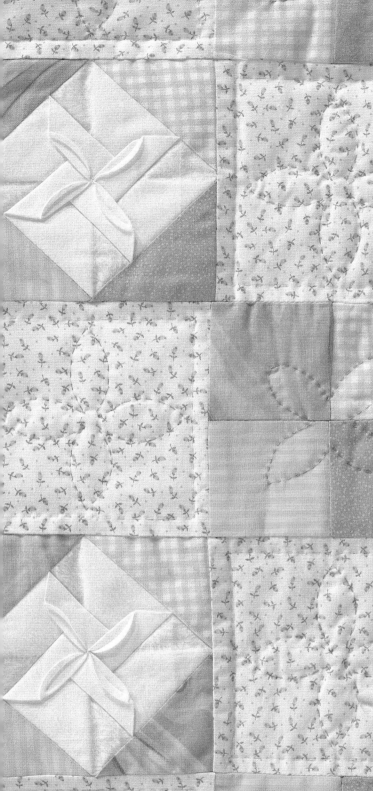

CHAPTER 2

Diamond Variations

*T*he origami block with a diamond shape in the center introduced in Stars, page 10, step 9 provides a base on which different shapes and designs can be formed. Experiment by folding and twisting the diamond with different angles: you will see the various shapes you can make. Manipulate the diamond shape with a few stitches to hold different parts of the diamond together: you will see even more variations. Now that you know how to fold the diamond block, you will be able to create the blocks introduced here. The new element is to hold all the midpoints on the four sides of the diamond with a few stitches. These diamond variations are fun to make.

1. Refer to Steps A and B of the Folding Instructions in Stars, pages 9-10.

2. Insert a needle from the back of the fabric to the center of the diamond.

3. Insert the needle to pick up a little bit of fabric from one side of the diamond at the center of the folded edge.

4. Rotate the fabric clockwise 90° and repeat Step 3.

5. Repeat Step 4 on the remaining two sides.

6. Pull the thread to gather all the four midpoints.

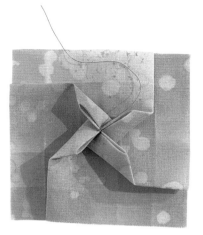

7. Finger-press the center slightly to form a propeller shape. Stitch to secure the center.

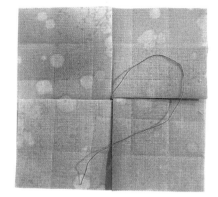

8. Make a knot at the back of the block.

9. Variation A: No further pressing is needed.

10. Variation B: Open each propeller leaf and iron-press to set the shape. Tack the leaves, if you plan to machine wash the quilt.

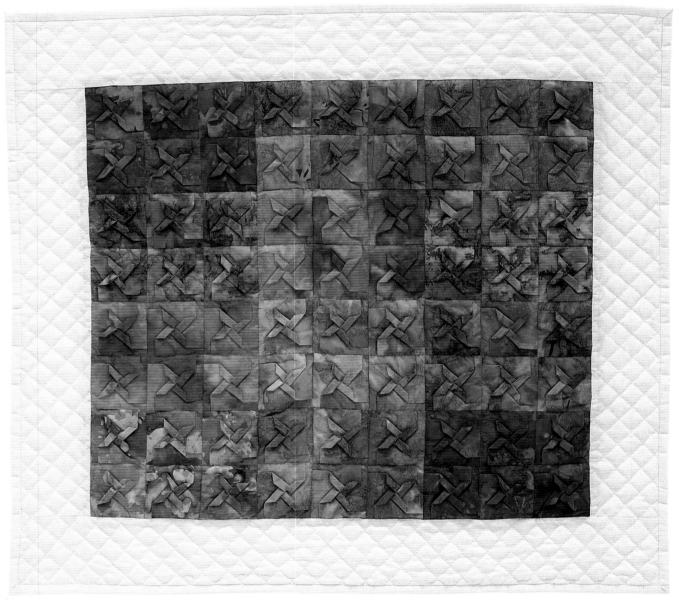

Paint Brush Basin—Variation A, 38³/₄" x 35¹/₂", Rebecca Wat

𝒟imension and rich colors make *Paint Brush Basin* an eye-catching quilt. The folded squares, which form the quilt, can be easily modified to any size. The many three-dimensional propeller shapes remind me of the moment when a painter lifts a paintbrush off a basin of thick, colorful paints. Use your imagination as to what is being painted.

Materials

Folded Blocks: Seven different fabrics are used here.

Five fabrics: $1/2$ yard each

Two fabrics: $1/4$ yard each

Border and Binding: $1 1/4$ yards

Backing: $1 1/4$ yards

Batting: 40" x 43"

Cutting

Folded Blocks:

◆ From each of the five $1/2$ yard fabrics, cut two 6"-wide strips, then cut strips into 6" squares. You will need 12 squares of each fabric.

◆ From each of the two $1/4$ yard fabrics, cut one 6"-wide strip, then cut strip into 6" squares. You will need 6 squares of each fabric.

Borders and Binding: Refer to page 85 for help cutting correct lengths, if needed.

◆ Border: Cut four 5"-wide strips lengthwise.

◆ Binding: Cut four $3 1/4$"-wide strips lengthwise.

To make binding refer to pages 87-88.

Folding

Fold and finger-press each 6" square following steps shown in the Folding Instructions for Variation A, pages 18-19. Each folded square should measure $3 3/4$".

Construction

1. Lay all the squares onto a flat surface. Refer to the quilt for design arrangement. Sew the squares together in rows. Press the seam allowances of each row in an alternate direction. This will make matching seams easier.

2. Join the rows together, matching seams. Press seams in one direction.

3. Attach the side borders first, then the top and bottom borders. Press seams toward borders.

4. Refer to pages 86-88 for general quilting and finishing instructions.

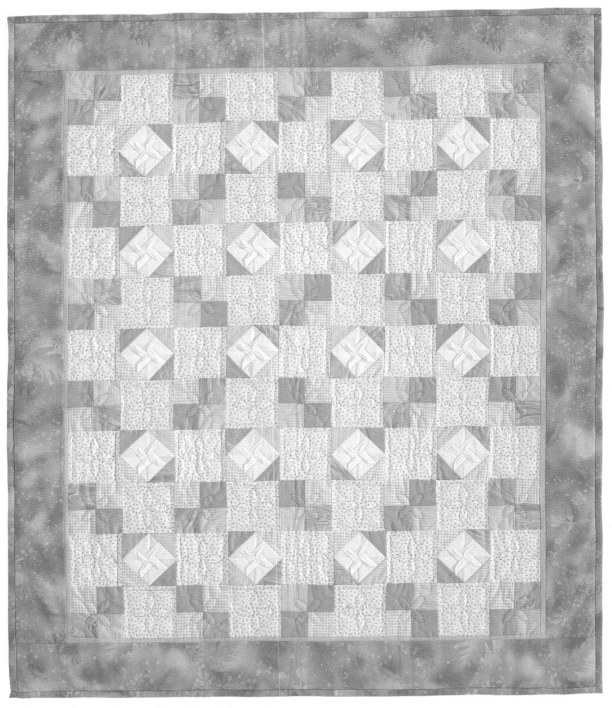

Baby's Breath—Variation B, 45¹/₂" x 53¹/₂", Rebecca Wat

This origami block, with a tiny little flower in the center (Variation B) has such a delicate and gentle look that I was inspired to design a baby quilt. Three colors—white, light yellow, and light green—express the feeling of softness and gentleness. You can easily replace the yellow or green with other soft colors.

Materials

Folded Flowers: 1 yard
Background and Four-Patch Blocks: four (A, B, C, D)
    fabrics: $3/8$ yard each
Alternate Block: 1 yard
Inner Border: $1/4$ yard
Outer Border and Binding: $1^2/3$ yards
Backing: $3^1/4$ yards
Batting: 50" x 58"

Cutting

Folded Flowers: Cut four strips $7^1/4$"-wide, then cut strips into $7^1/4$" squares. You will need 20 squares.

Background and Four-Patch Blocks: From each of the four (A, B, C, D) fabrics, cut four $2^1/2$"-wide strips. Then use one and a quarter strips of each fabric to cut $2^1/2$" squares. You will need 20 squares of each fabric. Save the partial and the remaining strips for the Four-Patch block construction.

Alternate Blocks: Cut seven $4^1/2$"-wide strips, then cut strips into $4^1/2$" squares. You will need 49 squares.

Borders and Binding: Refer to page 85 for help cutting correct lengths, if needed.
◆ Inner Border: Cut five 1"-wide strips (You will need to piece strips together end-to-end and cut to the required length for your quilt.)
◆ Outer Border: Cut four $4^1/2$"-wide strips lengthwise.
◆ Binding: Cut four $3^1/4$"-wide strips lengthwise. To make binding refer to pages 87-88.

Folding

Fold and finger-press twenty $7^1/4$" squares following the steps shown in the Folding Instructions for Variation B, pages 18-19. Each folded square should measure $4^1/2$".

Construction

1. Fold each of eighty $2^1/2$" squares (20 each of fabrics A, B, C, D) in half diagonally to form a crease, or draw a line with a marking tool. This is the stitching line for piecing it to the folded flower square.

2. Sew four $2^1/2$" squares onto the corners of each $4^1/2$" folded flower square as shown. Trim off excess fabrics underneath the corners. Press.

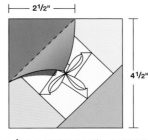

Sewing squares onto corners

3. To make Four-Patch blocks, sew the $2^1/2$"-wide strips of A and B fabrics together. Sew the $2^1/2$"-wide strips of C and D fabrics together. (Make sure one strip is light and one strip is dark.) Press. Cut the resulting $4^1/2$"-wide sets apart every $2^1/2$", as shown. You will need 30 AB units and 30 CD units.

Four-Patch block construction

Cut sewn strips into $2^1/2$" units

Sew AB unit to CD unit. Press.

4. Refer to the quilt and lay all the squares out on a flat surface. Sew them together into rows or sections. Press the seam allowances of each row in an alternate direction. This will make matching seams easier.

5. Join the rows or sections together, matching seams. Press seams in one direction.

6. Attach the side inner borders first, then the top and bottom inner borders. Press seams toward borders. Repeat for the outer border.

7. Refer to pages 86-88 for general quilting and finishing instructions.

Inside–Out Flowers

*T*he inside-out flower is one of the most exciting fabric origami designs that I have created. Four three-dimensional folded petals against a square background give the impression of an eight-petaled flower. Despite its complicated appearance, the origami block itself is quite easy to make and can be used like any other square in a patchwork quilt.

The most fascinating part of making this origami block is that you make the flower bloom with your own hands by turning the petals inside-out one-by-one. When working on *Springtime Impression* I, my first quilt using this design, I saved this flower-opening part until the quilt was basted. When I finally made the flowers bloom one-by-one, I was so excited that I could hear my heart beating. This process was a rewarding experience. May you experience the same joy and excitement when using this design in your own project.

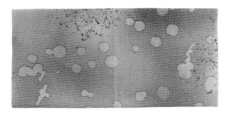

1. With the fabric wrong-side up, fold the square in half horizontally. Finger-press to make a crease along the fold line. Repeat for the vertical fold.

2. Open the fabric (wrong-side up). Bring one corner up to align with the intersection of the finger-pressed creases, then fold and finger-press.

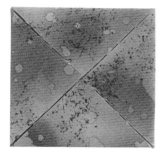

3. Repeat Step 2 on the remaining sides of the fabric.

4. Turn the block over. Bring the bottom edge up to align with the intersection of the creases in the center. Finger-press the fold, and then unfold.

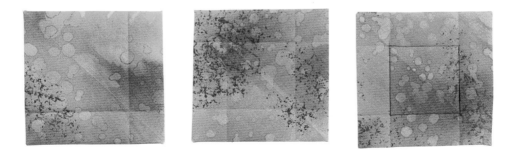

5. Create a square in the center by rotating the block and repeating Step 4 on the remaining sides.

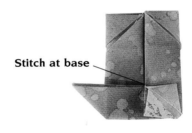

6. Using the crease lines as guidelines, bring two adjacent bottom edges to the center to form an "ear" between them.

7. Repeat Step 6 on the remaining sides while stitching the base of the "ears" together as you go.

Stitch at base

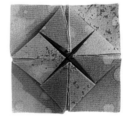

8. Flip the four side-triangles from the back to the front.

9. Iron-press to set the shape. This folded square can now be pieced into the quilt or garment.

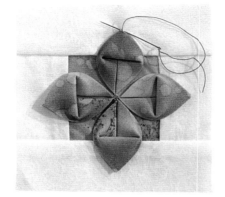

10. After the blocks are sewn in place, turn the "ears" inside out to form four petals. Turn fabrics at the tips of the petals under and stitch the petals in place. (You only need to tack down the tips of the petals.)

Springtime Impression I

Springtime Impression I, 61" x 61", Rebecca Wat

Springtime is a time when everything is fresh, new, and bright. It is these attributes of spring that set the tone of *Springtime Impression I*. Parades of flowers in bright, cheerful colors bloom and dance among green bushes, refreshed by the touch of a gentle shower. That is my first impression of spring.

Materials

Folded Flowers: ³/₈ yard each of 11 colorful fabrics
Background:
   White: 1²/₃ yards
   Green: 1 yard
Border and Binding: 2 yards
Backing: 3³/₄ yards
Batting: 65" x 65"

Cutting

Folded Flower Nine-Patches:

◆ From each of the 11 colorful fabrics, cut two 6"-wide strips, then cut strips into 6" squares. You will need 125 squares.
◆ From white background, cut eight 3"-wide strips, then cut strips into 3" squares. You will need 100 squares.

Nine-Patches:

◆ From white background, cut ten 3"-wide strips.
◆ From green background, cut eight 3"-wide strips.

Border and Binding: Refer to page 85 for help cutting correct lengths, if needed.

◆ Border: Cut four 4¹/₂"-wide strips lengthwise.
◆ Binding: Cut four 3¹/₄"-wide strips lengthwise. To make binding refer to pages 87-88.

Folding

Fold and finger-press each 6" square following steps shown in the Folding Instructions, pages 25-26. Each folded square should measure 3". If you plan to quilt in-the-ditch, do not turn the petals inside out until you have finished quilting; otherwise, open the petals after the quilt top is pieced together.

Construction

1. For the green and white Nine-Patch blocks: Arrange the strips in order and sew three strips in alternate colors together, as shown. Press seam allowances toward the green strip(s). After sewing the strips together, cut them into 3"-wide units. You will need 48 of unit 1 and 24 of unit 2 to make 24 Nine-Patch blocks.

Strip piecing the Nine-Patches

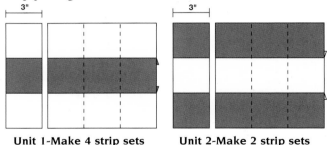

Unit 1-Make 4 strip sets   Unit 2-Make 2 strip sets

2. Sew the units for Block A together as shown below to form 24 Nine-Patch blocks. Press.

3. Sew together 25 of Block B, as shown. When sewing squares together, take care not to stretch or pull open the 3-D flower squares. Press.

Block construction

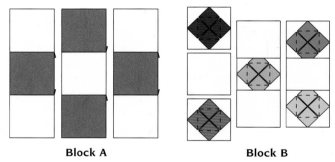

Block A   Block B

4. Arrange and sew the blocks together into rows as shown in the quilt. Press seam allowances of each row in an alternate direction. This will make matching the seams easier.

5. Join the rows together, matching seams. Press seams in one direction.

6. Attach the mitered borders. Refer to pages 85-86 for further instructions, if needed.

7. Open the flowers following Step 10 of the Folding Instructions, page 26.

8. Refer to pages 86-88 for general quilting and finishing instructions.

Springtime Impression II

Springtime Impression II, 29" x 29", Rebecca Wat

$\mathcal{V}$ery soft pastel colors are used to interpret the more subtle side of spring in *Springtime Impression* II. Flowers in the garden peek through the windows; drops of water, formed by the morning mist hang tight on the cheeks of the flowers. That is also my impression of spring.

Materials

Folded Flowers: 1/4 yard each of four colors
Background: 1/3 yard
Sashing: 1/3 yard
Border and Binding: 1 yard (Buy extra for Step 5.)
Backing: 1 yard
Batting: 33" x 33"
Embroidery ribbons and 16 pearl-like buttons

Cutting

Folded Flowers: Cut one 6"-wide strip from each color, then cut each strip into 6" squares. You will need 4 squares of each color, 16 squares total.

Background:
◆ Cut two 1½"-wide strips, then cut the strips into 1½" squares (A), and 1½" x 3" rectangles (B). You will need 4 (A) squares and 16 (B) rectangles.
◆ Cut two 3"-wide strips, then cut the strips into 3" x 6½" rectangles (C), and 3" x 9" rectangles (D). You will need 4 (C) rectangles and 4 (D) rectangles.

Sashing: Cut four 2"-wide strips for the sashing, then from two of the strips cut a 9" and a 22" length. You will need two 9" and two 22" lengths. Cut three 19" lengths from the remaining two strips.

Borders and Binding: Refer to page 85 for help cutting correct lengths, if needed.
◆ Borders: Cut four 4"-wide strips. These can be cut lengthwise or crosswise depending on the fabric design.
◆ Binding: Cut four 3¼"-wide strips. To make binding refer to pages 87-88.

Folding

Fold and finger-press each 6" square following the steps shown in the Folding Instructions, pages 25-26. The folded squares should measure 3". Do not turn the petals inside out until the quilt top is pieced together.

Construction

1. First sew a 1½" x 3" rectangle (B) to each folded flower square. Then sew one unit to the center 1½" square (A) and continue attaching units as you would for a Log Cabin block. For the last unit you will have to stop, or pivot, to make a right angle seam. Press.

Sew the 3" x 6½" rectangle (C), then the 3" x 9" rectangle (D) to complete the block. Press. Repeat to make three more blocks.

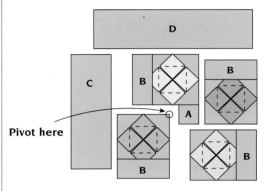

Block construction

2. Sew the 9" vertical sashing strips to join the blocks into two rows. Press. Sew the 19" horizontal sashing strips on top, center, and bottom of the blocks. Press. Sew the 22" vertical sashing strips on the sides. Press.

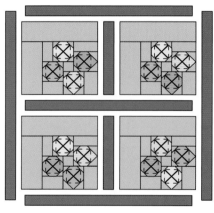

Quilt construction

3. Attach the side borders first, then the top and bottom borders. Press seams toward the borders.

4. Open the flowers following Step 10 of the Folding Instructions, page 26.

5. You may choose, as I did, to appliqué motifs cut from the border fabric to overlap the sashing and border. See page 85, for appliqué instructions, if needed.

6. Refer to pages 86-88 for general quilting and finishing instructions

Inside-Out Flower Vest

Inside-Out Flower Vest, Rebecca Wat

This vest is my experiment using the inside-out flower design on a garment. The process is smooth and painless. You just need to replace a portion of a garment by incorporating the inside-out flowers. After understanding the idea, you can apply this to a variety of sewing projects.

Materials

A simple commercial pattern for a loose-fitting vest
Amount of fabric indicated on the pattern plus
$^5/_8$ yard to make bias binding and alternate blocks. If you prefer, you can purchase pre-made bias binding. (You will need to measure your vest pattern to determine how much bias binding you need.)
Amount of lining and thin batting indicated on the pattern
Folded Flowers: $^1/_3$ yard
Number of buttons indicated on the pattern

Cutting

Pattern Preparation: Choose the right size from the pattern. Consider using the next larger size since heavy quilting will slightly reduce the size of the finished garment.

You can either cut on the stitching line of the correct size, adding $^5/_8$" to side and shoulder seams. Or if you prefer, trace the **stitching line** of the correct size on a piece of tracing paper, adding $^5/_8$" seam allowances at the side and shoulder seams. Then cut the pattern from the tracing paper.

Vest:
◆ Using the pattern as a guide, cut out the fronts and back of the vest from the fabric, lining, and batting.
◆ Cut one 2"-wide strip of vest fabric, then cut strip into 2" squares. Start with 12 squares, depending on the size of the vest you may need to cut a few additional squares.
◆ Cut one $3^1/_2$" x 12" piece of vest fabric.

Folded Flowers: Cut two 4"-wide strips, then cut strips into 4" squares. Start with 12 squares, depending on the size of the vest you may need to cut a few additional squares for the folded flowers.

Binding: The exact amount needed will depend on the size and style of the vest.

Folding

Fold and finger-press each 4" square following the steps shown in the Folding Instructions, pages 25-26. The folded blocks should measure 2". Do not turn the petals inside out until both sides of the vest front are pieced.

Construction

1. Mark and cut a $2^1/2$"-wide strip from each vest front as shown.

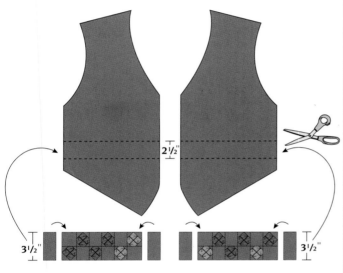

Inserting flowers into vest

2. Using a $1/4$" seam allowance, sew the 2" squares and the folded flowers together to create two strips, one for each vest front, as shown above. Press.

3. From the $3^1/2$" x 12" piece of vest fabric, cut and sew additional lengths onto each end of the strips created from the previous step. Match the length of the strips cut from both sides of the original vest front. This will provide room for the buttons at the center front. You can omit or add flower strips as needed. Press.

4. Using a $1/4$" seam allowance, sew the strips to both vest fronts. Press.

5. Turn the petals of the flowers inside out and stitch in place.

6. Pin or baste the three layers (vest, batting, and lining) together.

7. Quilt along the pattern of fabric or any way you desire.

8. Using a $5/8$" seam allowance and a shorter stitch length, sew the shoulder seams and side seams right-sides together.

9. Cut excess seam allowances from shoulder seams and side seams, leaving no more than $1/4$" remaining. Press the seams open. Cover them with bias binding and blind stitch in place as shown on page 89.

10. Pin and sew binding onto the right side of the armholes and outer edges of vest. Turn the binding over the raw edges of the vest. Blind stitch onto the lining side.

11. Make buttonholes and sew on buttons.

CHAPTER 4

Folded Roses

*T*he three-dimensional folded rose is the first fabric origami I created. While embodying the characteristics and dimensions that clearly resemble a rose, its interlocking petals are arranged in a way that makes it an easy-to-work-with appliqué.

It did not take me long to discover the tremendous possibilities this design possesses. I started out making dozens of roses and hand-stitching them onto a piece of fabric to create a quilt top. Then I found an old flower-basket pattern and replaced all the flowers with my roses. In fact, this design is so versatile that it can be applied to many areas other then quilting. You can make roses in different colors and sizes, and appliqué them onto pillows, table runners, napkins, or simply glue them onto decorative boxes, picture frames, etc. And of course, another possibility is to make a vest like the one shown on page 42.

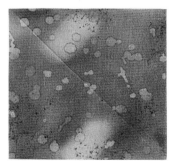

1. With the fabric wrong-side up, fold the square in half to form a triangle. Finger-press to make a crease along the fold line.

2. Open the fabric. Repeat Step 1 on another side to form an intersection in the center.

3. Bring one raw edge up to align with the fold line in the center. Finger-press to make a crease.

4. Open the fabric. Bring the adjacent raw edge up to align with the same fold line in Step 3. Finger-press to make a crease.

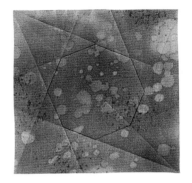

5. Repeat Steps 3 and 4 three on the remaining corners so that an octagon is formed in the center. (This is the base of the rose).

6. Bring two adjacent raw edges up to align with the diagonal crease in the center forming an "ear" between them. Finger-press the "ear" to the upper side.

7. Tuck under the raw edge of the "ear" formed in the previous step, while bringing the bottom raw edge up to align with the crease in the center. Finger-press.

8. Bring the next bottom edge up to align with the diagonal crease in the center, forming an "ear" between itself and the previous adjacent bottom edge. Finger-press the "ear" to the left

9. Rotate the block clockwise 90° and repeat Step 7.

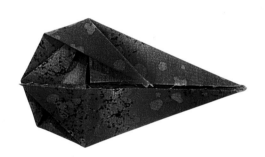

10. Bring the next bottom edge up to align with the horizontal crease in the center, forming an "ear" between itself and the previous adjacent bottom edge. Finger-press the "ear" to the left.

11. Repeat Step 7.

12. Finger-press the last "ear" and tuck it under the "ear" formed in the previous step. Iron-press to set the shape.

Center of the Rose

Create a fabric center, described in the following steps. This is a short cut to form the diamond block on pages 9-10. If you prefer, you can go back and follow those instructions for the same result.

13. Cut a 2" square. With right-side up, fold the square in half horizontally and then vertically. Finger-press to form creases. Turn the block wrong-side up.

14. With wrong-side up, pick up the creased intersection and twist it to the right.

15. Adjust the center to form a diamond shape. Iron-press. (Note that the size of the finished block doesn't have to be exact).

16. Turn block over with right-side up. Iron-press to set the shape.

17. Insert the block created in Step 16 into the center of the rose.

18. Stitch from the back to secure both the center and all four corners of the inserted block, catching every layer except the top.

Three Topiaries

Three Topiaries, 50" x 38", Rebecca Wat, quilted by Virginia Dunlap

This is a lovely way to incorporate topiaries within quilting. The quilt shows three charming topiaries sitting elegantly at the window, each with a different shape, covered with roses in matching colors. A generous use of three-dimensional folded roses, partially overlapping each other, creates an effect that is difficult to achieve through the use of single-dimensional appliqué. The border, designed to resemble a window-frame, adds depth to the whole picture. The whimsical spiral designs in the background further enhance the contemporary look.

Since there are three topiary designs, you may choose to make a smaller quilt by doing only one or two of them. Another alternative is to use the same ideas to create topiaries in the forms and shapes of your own choice. In any case, you will end up with a very unique piece.

Materials

Folded Roses: 5/8 yard each of three colors
Flowerpots: 1/4 yard
Leaves: 1/8 yard
Stems: 1/8 yard
Background: 1 yard
Side Borders: 1/3 yard crosswise
 Or 1 1/4 yards lengthwise, depending on fabric design
Top and Bottom Borders and Binding: 1 1/2 yards
 lengthwise
Backing: 1 3/4 yards
Batting: 42" x 54"
Bow: 2 1/2 yards of ribbon
Yarns for the moss and decorative designs in the
 background
Leaf template pattern on page 90

Cutting

Folded Roses:
◆ Cut twelve 3 1/2"-wide strips, then cut strips into 3 1/2" squares. You will need 130 squares.
◆ Cut seven 2"-wide strips, then cut strips into 2" squares. You will need 130 squares.

Flower Pots:
◆ Cut three 7 1/2" x 9" pieces for the pots.
◆ Cut three 2" x 10" pieces for the pot rims.

Leaves: Using template, trace and cut eighteen leaves, adding 3/16" seam allowance if you want to hand appliqué.

Stems: Finished width of stems is 1/2". Cut one strip 7/8"-wide if hand appliquéing, or 1/2"-wide if machine appliquéing.

Background: Cut one piece 41 1/2" x 31 1/2".

Side Borders: Cut two 5" x 41" strips (extra length allows for mitered corners).

Top Border: Cut one 3" x 54" strip (extra length allows for mitered corners).

Bottom Border: Cut one 4" x 54" strip (extra length allows for mitered corners).

Binding: Cut four 3 1/4"-wide strips. To make binding refer to pages 87-88.

Folding

1. Fold and finger-press the 3 1/2" squares into three-dimensional roses, and the 2" squares for the centers following the steps shown in the Folding Instructions, pages 34-36.

2. Make three flowerpots. With wrong side up, fold along the fold lines indicated.

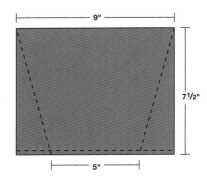

With wrong side up, fold 1/4" along all edges of the 2" x 10" piece.

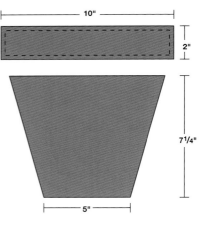

With right side up, cover the top of the pot with the piece.

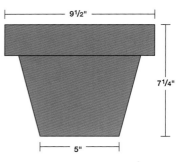

Construction

1. Sew borders to the background fabric. Refer to Adding Mitered Borders, page 86.

2. Arrange all the flowerpots and stem appliqués (cut to desired length) on the background fabric. Pin or baste them before hand or machine appliquéing.

3. Arrange the roses on the background fabric. Pin or baste them before hand appliquéing.

4. Mark the whimsical designs in the background with a marking tool and sew the designs by hand or machine using your favorite decorative stitch.

5. Pin and appliqué the leaves in position.

6. To make moss in the flower pots, arrange the yarns in position and sew by machine to secure.

7. Pin and tack the bow in position.

8. Refer to pages 86-88, for general quilting and finishing instructions.

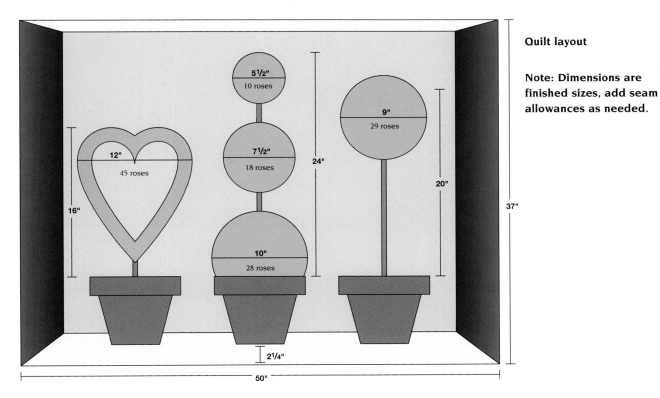

Quilt layout

Note: Dimensions are finished sizes, add seam allowances as needed.

Baskets of Roses

Baskets of Roses, 51¹/₂" x 51¹/₂", Rebecca Wat

As I mentioned earlier, *Baskets of Roses* is an adaptation of Flower Baskets, a traditional block. I view this quilt as an experiment to renew the look of a traditional design by adding new elements—the three-dimensional folded roses. This can become your experiment too. The size and color of the roses, as well as the way they are arranged in this quilt, are merely suggestions. Try different colors or arrangements, or add other kinds of flowers to create that unique look you have in mind.

Materials

Folded Roses: A variety to total 1¹/₂ yards (three different colors were used in example).

Leaves: scraps of a variety of greens or ¹/₈ yard of one green

Baskets:

    Fabric A (dark): ³/₈ yard

    Fabric B (light): ¹/₃ yard

Background (white): ³/₄ yard

Alternate Blocks (green): ³/₄ yard

Corner Triangles: 1⁵/₈ yards

Binding: ³/₄ yard crosswise

    Or 1³/₄ yards lengthwise

Backing: 3 yards

Batting: 56" x 56"

Small and Large Leaf Patterns on page 90

Cutting

Folded Roses:

◆ Cut 43 squares ranging from 4" to 5".

◆ Cut four 6¹/₂" squares for large roses on the corners.

◆ Cut four 4" squares to make 4 small roses for tucking inside the centers of the large roses.

◆ Cut forty-seven 2" squares for the centers of the roses.

Baskets:

◆ Cut three 4¹/₈"-wide strips from fabric A, then cut strips into nineteen 4¹/₈" squares. Cut the squares diagonally twice into 76 triangles (need 75 to make five baskets).

◆ Cut three 2⁷/₈"-wide strips from fabric B, then cut strips into 30 squares. Cut the squares diagonally into 60 triangles. This will make 5 baskets.

Background (white):

◆ Cut one 4⁷/₈"-wide strip, then cut strip into three 4⁷/₈" squares. Cut the squares diagonally into 6 triangles (only need 5).

◆ Cut three 2¹/₂"-wide strips, then cut strips into ten 2¹/₂" x 8¹/₂" rectangles.

◆ Cut one 10⁷/₈"-wide strip, then cut into three 10⁷/₈" squares. Cut the squares diagonally into 6 triangles (only need 5).

Alternate Blocks: Cut four 12¹/₂" squares.

Corner Triangles: Cut two 26³/₈" squares, then cut diagonally. You will need 4 triangles.

Binding: Cut six 3¹/₄"-wide crosswise strips, or four 3¹/₄"-wide lengthwise strips. Refer to pages 87-88 to make binding.

Folding

Fold 43 roses for the blocks and corners. Fold 4 larger roses. Fold 4 smaller roses to put inside the large roses following steps shown in the Folding Instructions pages 34-35. Fold the forty-seven 2" squares for the centers of the roses, page 36.

Construction

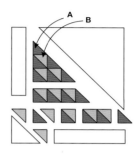

1. Piece the Basket blocks together as shown. Press.

2. Sew the alternate blocks and the Basket blocks together into rows. Press toward the alternate blocks.

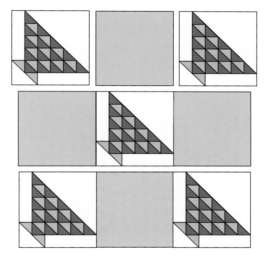

3. Join rows together matching seams. Press.

4. Make sure that your quilt top is square and measures 36¹/₂" on each side.

5. Add the 4 corner triangles to the sides of the quilt top. Press toward the corner triangles.

6. Trace and cut 15 small leaf appliqués for the blocks and 8 large leaf appliqués for the corners. Add ³/₁₆" turn-under allowance, if hand appliquéing.

7. Arrange and pin the roses and leaves, then appliqué.

8. Refer to pages 86-88, for general quilting and finishing instructions.

Vest of Roses

Vest of Roses, Rebecca Wat

$\mathcal{I}$f you like roses, how about wearing a vest full of them? This vest, covered with hand-folded red roses, is an expression of my fantasy and passion for this beautiful flower. It looks elegant and different, and is fun to wear, especially on Valentine's Day. In addition, it provides a good opportunity for you to show off your fabric-folding skills.

Materials

A simple commercial pattern for a loose-fitting vest.
Amount of fabric indicated on the pattern plus ¹/₂ yard to make binding. If you prefer, you can purchase pre-made bias binding. (You will need to measure your vest pattern to determine how much bias binding you need.)
Amount of lining indicated on the pattern.
Folded Roses: A variety to total 2 yards
Number of buttons indicated on the pattern.

Cutting

Pattern Preparation: Choose the right size from the pattern. You can either cut on the stitching line of the correct size, adding ⁵/₈" to side and shoulder seams. Or if you prefer, trace the **stitching line** of the correct size on a piece of tracing paper, adding ⁵/₈" seam allowances at the side and shoulder seams. Then cut the pattern from the tracing paper.

Vest: Using the pattern as a guide, cut out the fronts and back of the vest from the fabric and lining.

Folded Roses: Cut 66 squares ranging from 4" to 5". Cut sixty-six 2" squares for centers.

Binding: The exact amount needed will depend on the size and style of the vest.

Folding

Fold and finger-press the 66 squares for the roses and the 66 squares for the rose centers following the steps shown in the Folding Instructions, pages 34-36.

Construction

1. Lay out and pin the roses in desired position. Hand appliqué them to the vest fronts.

2. Using a ⁵/₈" seam allowance, sew the shoulder seams and side seams of the top-layer right-sides together. Press the seams open.

3. Using a ⁵/₈" seam allowance, sew the shoulder seams and side seams of the lining right-sides together. Press the seams open.

4. Pin vest and lining wrong-sides together, matching shoulder seams and side seams, neckline, and front and bottom edges. Pin and sew bias binding onto the vest fabric. Turn the binding over the raw edge to the inside of the vest. Blind stitch onto the lining side.

5. Make buttonholes and sew on buttons.

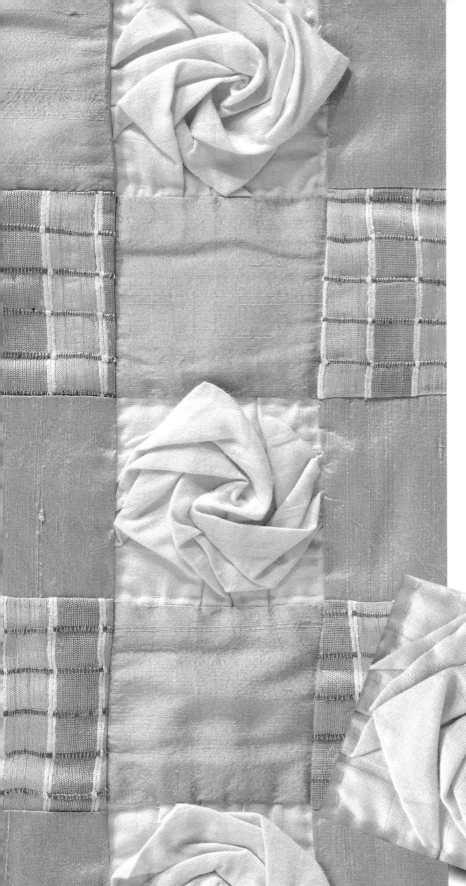

Twirled Roses

*T*he origami block introduced in this chapter is the patchwork version of a three-dimensional rose. You may be surprised that a simple folding technique such as pleats is responsible for creating vivid and stylish three-dimensional roses. You will probably be even more surprised to find out that a whole block or even a whole quilt top full of roses can be created out of a single piece of fabric by using this technique. And if you are patient and skillful enough, perhaps you can make someone special a wedding gown with a train full of these roses.

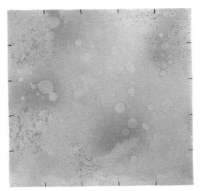

1. Take a 5" square, with right-side up, divide the width of each side into five parts and mark them. These marks are 1" apart and are called placement lines. Divide the center three 1" spaces into thirds. These will be the fold lines. If a larger block is used, divide it into five equal parts for the placement lines. Divide the center three parts into thirds to create the fold lines.

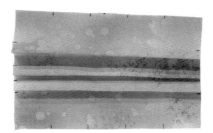

2. Using the marks as guidelines, bring the two-thirds' fold lines up to the 1" placement lines, making three pleats in the center, each measuring one-third of an inch deep. Iron-press to set the pleats.

3. Repeat Step 2 vertically to form a 3" square.

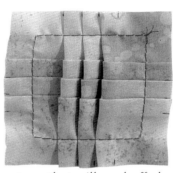

4. Using any tape that will peel off clean, tape or pin the pleats, then baste them in position about ³/₈" from the edge. Remove the tape or pins.

5. Pull the pleats open. Pinch and hold the center of the "pouf" of opened pleats with two fingers. With another hand, rotate the block in the same direction as many times as you can.

6. Adjust the pleats to form the shape of a rose by holding the center while pulling the outer edges to form petals. Iron-press to set the shape. Make a few stitches to keep the shape.

White Roses I

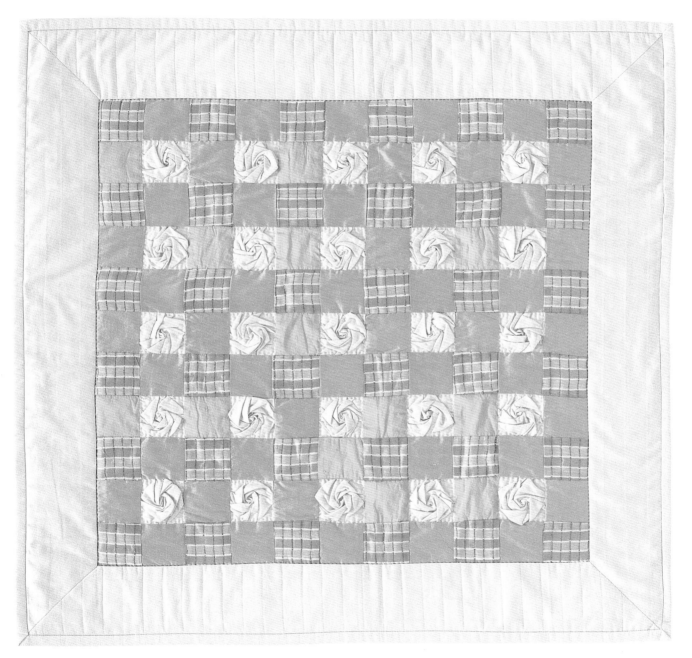

White Roses I, 36" x 36", Rebecca Wat

Simplicity and elegance are the look and feel of the White Roses series. *White Roses* I is a combination of three-inch squares in ivory, beige solid, and beige check fabrics. The dimensional twirled white roses are essential to this design because they give an otherwise ordinary quilt a touch of interest and beauty. Expand this quilt to any size you desire, and you will have an elegant wedding quilt.

Materials

Twirled Roses: ³/₄ yard
Beige Solid: ⁵/₈ yard
Beige Check or Plaid: ¹/₃ yard
Border and Binding: 1¹/₄ yards
Backing: 1¹/₄ yards
Batting: 40" x 40"

Cutting

Twirled Roses: Cut four 5"-wide strips, then cut strips into 5" squares. You will need 25 squares.

Beige Solid: Cut five 3"-wide strips. From two of the strips cut twenty-five 3" squares. Set aside the other three strips to use in Step 1.

Beige Check or Plaid:
◆ Cut three 3"-wide strips.
◆ Cut one 3" square.

Borders and Binding: Refer to page 85 for help cutting correct lengths, if needed.
◆ Borders: Cut four 4¹/₂"-wide strips lengthwise.
◆ Binding: Cut four 3¹/₄"-side strips. Refer to pages 87-88 to make binding.

Folding

Fold and finger-press each 5" square following steps shown in the Folding Instructions, page 44. When folding the pleats, do not make them too big because the folded square needs to be at least 3" x 3". You can trim your squares to this size if they turn out to be slightly larger.

Construction

1. Sew three sets of a 3"-wide beige solid strip and a 3"-wide beige check or plaid strip together. Then cut each strip set into 3" x 5¹/₂" rectangles. You will need 35 rectangles.

2. Refer to the quilt and arrange the squares of roses, 3" solid squares, and 3" strip-pieced rectangles on a flat surface. Sew the pieces together row by row. Press the seam allowances of each row in an alternate direction. (The alternately pressed seam allowances of the blocks should make matching the seams easier.)

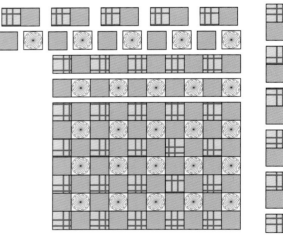

Quilt construction

3. Join the rows together, matching seams. Press in one direction.

4. Add the mitered borders. Refer to pages 85-86 for further instructions, if needed. Press seams toward borders.

5. Refer to pages 86-88 for general quilting and finishing instructions.

White Roses II

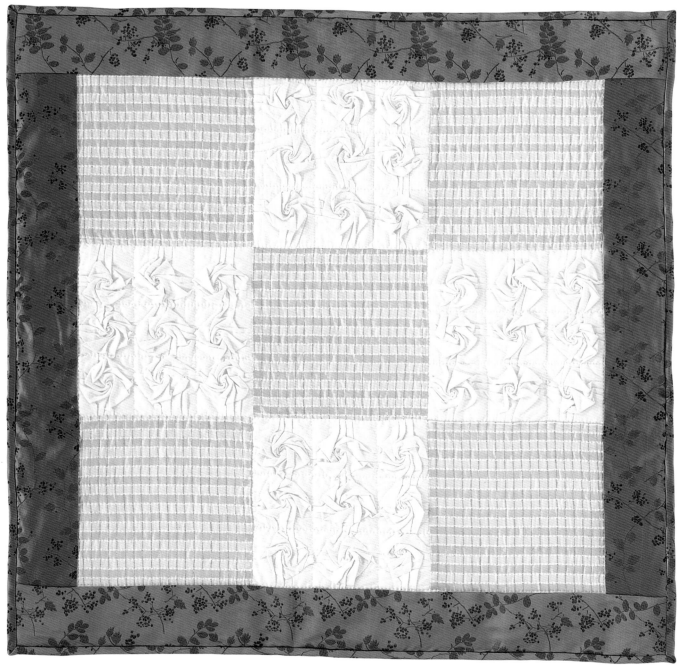

White Roses II, 38¹/₂" x 38¹/₂", Rebecca Wat

This White Rose quilt would make a beautiful wedding gift. The block arrangement is very simple—alternate blocks of twirled white roses and beige check fabric. Each nine-rose block is actually made from a single piece of fabric. Its dramatic effect reminds me of the art of sculpting. What would a quilt look like made entirely of dimensional twirled roses from one whole piece of fabric?

Materials

Twirled Roses: 1 yard
Alternate blocks: ³/4 yard
Borders and Binding: 1¹/4 yards
Backing: 1¹/4 yards
Batting: 43" x 43"

Cutting

Folded Roses: Cut four 17" squares.

Alternate Blocks: Cut five 10¹/2" squares.

Borders and Binding: Refer to page 85 for help cutting correct lengths, if needed.
◆ Borders: Cut four 4¹/2"-wide strips lengthwise.
◆ Binding: Cut four 3¹/4" strips lengthwise. Refer to pages 87-88 to make binding.

Folding

1. Mark the 17" squares as shown.

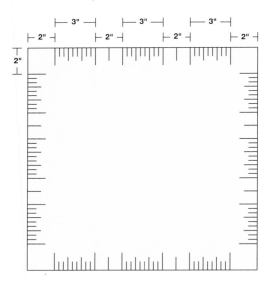

2. Fold the pleats for each block using the placement and fold lines.

3. Iron-press the pleats to set them in position. Tape the intersections of pleats down to secure their positions.

4. Baste to secure the positions of the pleats around the edges of the block and the intersections.

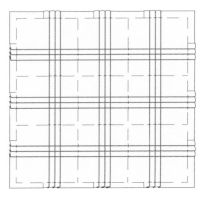

Basting the pleats

5. Remove the tape. Pull pleats open and form each of the 9 roses as described in the Folding Instructions, page 44.

6. Trim the blocks to 10¹/2", if needed.

Construction

1. Referring to the quilt, arrange the blocks on a flat surface. Sew the blocks together into rows. Press the seam allowances of each row in an alternate direction. (The alternately pressed seam allowances of the blocks should make matching the seams easier.)

2. Join the rows together, matching seams. Press in one direction.

3. Add the side borders first, then the top and bottom borders. Press seams toward the borders.

4. Refer to pages 86-88 for general quilting and finishing instructions.

Pinwheels

$\mathcal{T}$he Pinwheel block is an interesting design. It has an interlocking feature that is similar to that of the three-dimensional star, and yet its four seemingly revolving, outward-pointing triangles make it look very much like a pinwheel. I first came across this design while wrapping gifts, and I have since made many decorative boxes. After I started to make fabric origami blocks, I adapted this design and translated it into quilt patterns. One unique aspect is that it can be used either as an appliqué or as any other block in a patchwork quilt.

It is worth mentioning that using fabrics with stripes will add interesting effects, as illustrated by the pinwheel pillows shown in this chapter. You may also want to try combining fabrics of different colors together in different ways before folding.

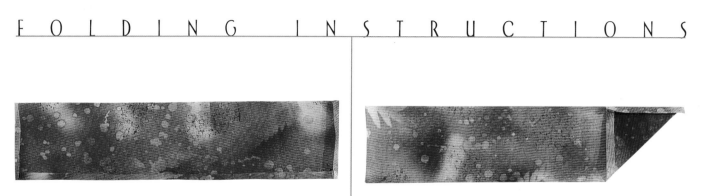

1. Cut a 4¹/₂" x 17¹/₂" rectangle (for a finished size of 4¹/₄" square) to use for practice folding. Follow cutting instructions in each project for correct size rectangle to use. With right-side up, fold in ¹/₄" on the bottom and the two side edges. Iron-press. (These are the seam allowances for this block).

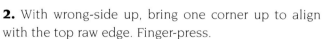

2. With wrong-side up, bring one corner up to align with the top raw edge. Finger-press.

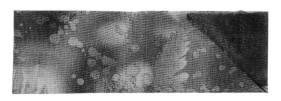

3. Flip the triangle formed in Step 2 to the left and finger-press.

4. Bring up the bottom right corner to align with the top raw edge. Finger-press.

5. Repeat Steps 3 and 4 to form crease lines as shown. Iron-press to form sharper creases if the creases formed by finger-pressing don't look sharp enough.

6. With right-sides together, sew the side edges using a ¹/₄" seam allowance.

Extra folding help for Step 7

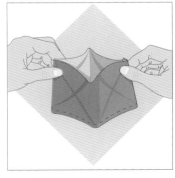

Grasp upper corners

Twist by bringing an upper corner down to lower corner

7. Turn the right side out. Stand the block up on its seam allowances. Grasp two upper opposite corners of the square with both hands and twist the block to the right, using the creases as guidelines. (This is similar to the interlocking feature at the bottom of some gift boxes.)

8. With seam allowances on the bottom, turn under the allowances at the four corners. Iron-press to set the shape.

9. Bring one corner up to align with the diagonal line in the center.

10. Rotate the square 90° clockwise. Repeat Step 9 on an adjacent corner, tucking the left-hand side under to hide the raw edges.

11. Repeat Step 10 on the next corner.

12. Rotate square 90° clockwise. Before bringing the last corner up to align with the central line, fold the raw edges of the previous triangle to the diagonal center line. They should be hidden after the last corner is turned up in the next step.

13. Bring the last corner up to align with the diagonal line in the center, tucking the left-hand side of the triangle under the previous triangle.

14. Stitch to secure the center of the pinwheel.

Playing with Pinwheels, 43¹/₂" x 43¹/₂", Rebecca Wat

W hile I was working on *Playing with Pinwheels*, I not only had fun working with the three-dimensional pinwheel design, but I also enjoyed mixing and matching fabrics of unusual colors, including metallics. I even sewed two strips of different fabrics together before folding the pinwheels to achieve a more complicated look. The resulting blocks look quite different. This wallhanging can easily fit into almost any room in the house.

Materials

Folded Pinwheels, Four-Patch Squares, and Side Triangles: a variety of colors totaling 1³/₄ yards
(The quilt pictured uses thirteen fabrics including one metallic. An average of ¹/₈ yard each will suffice.)
Background: 1¹/₄ yards
Border and Binding: 1³/₈ yards lengthwise
Backing: 2¹/₂ yards if fabric is less than 44" wide, otherwise 1¹/₃ yards will suffice.
Batting: 48" x 48"

Cutting

Folded Pinwheels: Cut thirteen 4¹/₂" x 17¹/₂" rectangles for the pinwheels. For a more complicated look, cut and sew together two rectangles each 2¹/₂" x 17¹/₂" so that the resulting size is 4¹/₂" x 17¹/₂".

Four Patches:
◆ Cut eight 2"-wide strips from background fabric.
◆ Cut eight 2"-wide strips from the variety of colorful fabrics.

Side Triangles: Cut ten 3⁷/₈" squares from various colors. Then cut squares in half diagonally. You will need 20 triangles.

Background: Cut four 3⁷/₈"-wide strips, then cut strips into thirty-six 3⁷/₈" squares. Cut squares in half diagonally. You will need 72 triangles.

Borders and Binding: Refer to page 85 for help cutting correct lengths, if needed.
◆ Borders: Cut four 4"-wide strips lengthwise.
◆ Binding: Cut four 3¹/₄"-wide strips lengthwise. Refer to pages 87-88 to make binding.

Folding

Make 13 pinwheels following steps as shown in the Folding Instructions, pages 51-53. The folded blocks should measure 4³/₄" square (seam allowances included).

Construction

1. To make the Four-Patch blocks, sew one 2"-wide strip of background fabric to a 2"-wide strip of colorful fabric. Press toward the darker color. Cut into 2" x 3¹/₂" rectangles. You will need 144 rectangles.

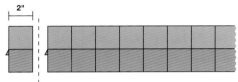

Strip piece the Four-Patch blocks

2. Sew the rectangular units together to make 72 single Four-Patch blocks. Press.

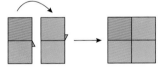

Single Four-Patch block construction

3. Sew 3⁷/₈" triangles (background fabric) to the four sides of the folded pinwheels to make thirteen 6¹/₂" blocks. Press.

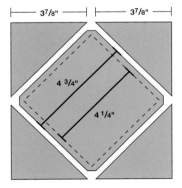

Block construction

4. Sew 20 background fabric triangles to 20 colorful fabric triangles creating 20 half-square triangle units. Press. Sew pairs of half-square triangle units together. Press.

Sewing triangles together

5. Referring to both the quilt and the quilt layout, arrange the pieces in the desired order.

6. Sew 2 Four-Patch blocks together to form 12 Half-Double Four-Patch blocks. Press.

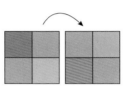

Half-Double Four-Patch block construction

7. Sew 4 Four-Patch blocks together to form 12 Double Four-Patch blocks

Double Four-Patch block construction

8. Sew blocks together into rows. Press seams open.

9. Join the rows together, matching seams. Press.

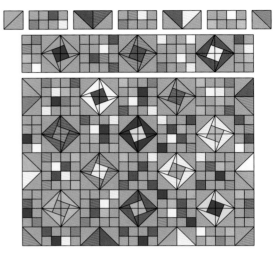

Quilt construction

10. Add the border strips concentrically around the quilt. Press seams toward the borders.

11. Refer to pages 86-88 for general quilting and finishing instructions.

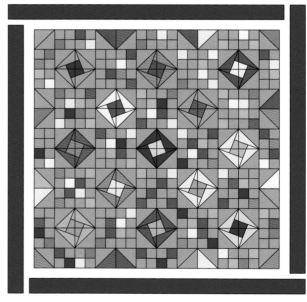

Attaching borders

Pinwheel Pillow

Pinwheel Pillow, 14"x14", Rebecca Wat

The three-dimensional pinwheel design can turn any ordinary looking square pillow into a unique conversation piece. The pillow shown is made of fabric with horizontal stripes. (Another alternative is to cut a vertical striped fabric crosswise.) You may want to use fabrics with different prints or combine different fabrics together, which can yield even more interesting results.

Materials

Folded Pillow: 1 yard

Note: If fabric is less than 44" in width and you want the pillow back in one piece, you should buy an additional $1/2$ yard of fabric.

Pillow form: 14"x 14"

Cording: $1^3/4$ yards

Cutting

Pinwheel: Either cut a piece of fabric measuring 57" x $14^1/2$" or sew two 29" x $14^1/2$" pieces together using a **$1/2$" seam allowance.**

Pillow Back: Cut (or piece together) one 15" square.

Folding

Fold the fabric as shown in the Folding Instructions, pages 51-53. Note: All seam allowances for pillow are $1/2$". The completed folded size of the pillow front should be 15" x 15". Press to set the form of the design.

Construction

1. Cut a piece of cording long enough to cover the four sides of the pillow. Sew the cording to the pillow front by hand or machine.

2. Sew the pillow front and pillow back together by hand while placing a 14" pillow form in-between. Alternatively, you can machine sew the pillow front and back right sides together, then turn it right-side out, and use the opening in the center of the pinwheel to insert the pillow form.

3. Stitch underneath the center of the pinwheel to secure the design of the pinwheel.

Polygon Flowers

*Y*ou can apply the folding techniques in this chapter to almost any polygon with equal sides. Pentagons, hexagons, octagons, etc. will turn into different types of flowers, such as morning glories, narcissus, sunflowers, and gerberas. The number of sides in a polygon determines the number of petals in each flower. For instance, octagons create flowers with eight petals. Each of the polygon flower designs introduced here has three-dimensional petals growing from a center decorated with a button. Alternatively, a simple round-shaped appliqué could be the center.

The three-dimensional hexagons introduced in this chapter are regular hexagons. All sides are equal in length and the angles between the sides are equal. This characteristic makes it possible to use the hexagon block just like any other regular hexagon in a patchwork quilt pattern, such as a Grandmother's Flower Garden. In this chapter there are actually two similar hexagon designs: the curved-petal hexagon and the diamond-petal hexagon, which are used in *My Flower Garden*.

Aside from quilting, these polygon flower designs can be used as appliqués for clothing and many home decorating items. After all, the delightful appearance of these polygon flowers will probably remind you of some unknown little flowers that you have seen along the roadside. So pick a polygon and create the flower you have in your mind.

Curved-Petal Hexagon

1. Trace 3" Hexagon template pattern, page 90, and cut a hexagon from fabric. With wrong-side up, fold the hexagon in half horizontally. Finger-press to make a crease along the fold line.

2. Open the fabric. Repeat Step 1 on the other two sides, forming three fold lines intersecting each other at the center.

3. Bring the bottom edge up to align with the finger-pressed crease in the center. Fold and finger-press.

4. Repeat Step 3 on the next side.

5. Repeat Step 3 on the remaining sides of the hexagon. When folding the last raw edge up, tuck excess fabric under its adjacent triangle to form six interlocking triangles.

6. Stitch to secure the center of the flower. Use a fray-prevention product on the flower centers if planning to machine wash your quilt. Open one side of the triangle and turn a little bit of the folded edge outward. Iron-press to set the shape.

7. Repeat Step 6 on the remaining sides. Cover the center with a button or an appliqué.

Diamond-Petal Hexagon

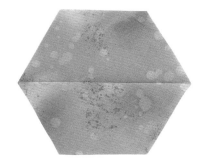

1. Trace 3" Hexagon template pattern, page 90, and cut a hexagon from fabric. With wrong-side up, fold the hexagon in half horizontally. Finger-press to make a crease along the fold line.

2. Open the fabric. Repeat Step 1 on the other two sides, forming three fold lines intersecting each other at the center.

3. Bring the bottom edge up to align with the finger-pressed crease in the center. Fold and finger-press. Open the fabric.

4. Repeat Step 3 on the remaining sides, forming a hexagon in the center.

5. Fold two adjacent raw edges toward the center, creating an "ear" between them.

6. Finger-press the "ear" to form a kite shape.

7. Open the kite shape and press all raw edges to the center to form a diamond shape. Finger-press.

8. Fold the tip of the diamond-shaped petal down to the center, covering the raw edges. Repeat Step 5 to create the next "ear".

9. Repeat Steps 5, 6, 7, and 8 on the remaining sides. Tack the central tips of the diamond shapes as you go from one side to another. Use a fray-prevention product on the flower centers if planning to machine wash your quilt.

10. Iron-press to set the shape. Cover the center with a button or an appliqué.

Pentagon Flowers

1. Trace 3¹/₄" Pentagon template pattern, page 91, and cut a pentagon from fabric. With wrong-side up, fold the pentagon in half horizontally, and then vertically, to form an intersection in the center.

2. Bring the bottom edge up to align with the intersection in the center. Fold and finger-press. Open the fabric.

3. Repeat Step 2 on the remaining sides, forming a pentagon in the center.

4. Fold two adjacent raw edges inward, creating an "ear" between them. Finger-press the "ear" to form a kite shape.

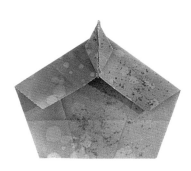

5. Open the kite shape and press all raw edges to the center to form a diamond shape. Finger-press.

6. Fold the tip of the diamond-shaped petal to the center, covering the raw edges. Tack the central tips of the diamond shapes as you go from one corner to another. Finger-press.

7. Repeat Steps 4, 5, and 6 on the remaining sides. Use a fray-prevention product on the flower centers if planning to machine wash your quilt.

8. Iron-press to set the shape. Cover the center with a button or an appliqué.

Octagon Flowers

1. Trace 2½" Octagon template pattern, page 91, and cut an octagon from fabric. With wrong-side up, fold the octagon in half horizontally. Open the fabric shape.

2. Bring the bottom edge up to align with the crease in the center. Fold and finger-press. Open the fabric shape.

3. Repeat Steps 1 and 2 on the remaining sides, forming an octagon in the center.

4. Fold two adjacent raw edges toward the center, creating an "ear" between them. Finger-press the "ear" to form a kite shape. Open the kite shape and press all raw edges to the center to form a diamond shape. Finger-press. Fold tip of diamond-shaped petal to center, covering the raw edges. (See page 62, Steps 4, 5, and 6 for forming and opening the kite shape.)

5. Repeat Step 4 on the remaining sides. Tack the central tips of the diamond shapes as you go from one side to another. Use a fray-prevention product on the flower centers if planning to machine wash your quilt.

6. Iron-press to set the shape. Cover the center with a button or an appliqué.

Twelve-Petal Flowers (Sunflower)

1. Trace 12-Sided Polygon template pattern, page 92, and cut a 12-sided polygon from fabric. With wrong-side up, fold the fabric in half horizontally. Open the fabric.

2. Bring the bottom edge up to align with the crease in the center. Fold and finger-press. Open the fabric shape.

3. Repeat Steps 1 and 2 on the remaining sides, forming a 12-sided polygon in the center. (It may help to outline the polygon with a pencil.)

4. Fold two adjacent raw edges toward the center, creating an "ear" between them. Finger-press the "ear" to form a kite shape. Open the kite shape and press all raw edges to the center to form a diamond shape. Finger-press. Fold tip of diamond-shaped petal to center, covering the raw edges. (See page 62, Steps 4, 5 and 6 for forming and opening the kite shape.)

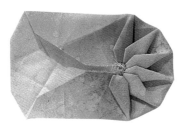

5. Repeat Step 4 on the remaining sides. Tack the central tips of the diamond shapes as you go from one side to another. Use a fray-prevention product on the flower centers if planning to machine wash your quilt.

6. Iron-press to set the shape. Cover the center with a button or an appliqué.

My Flower Garden

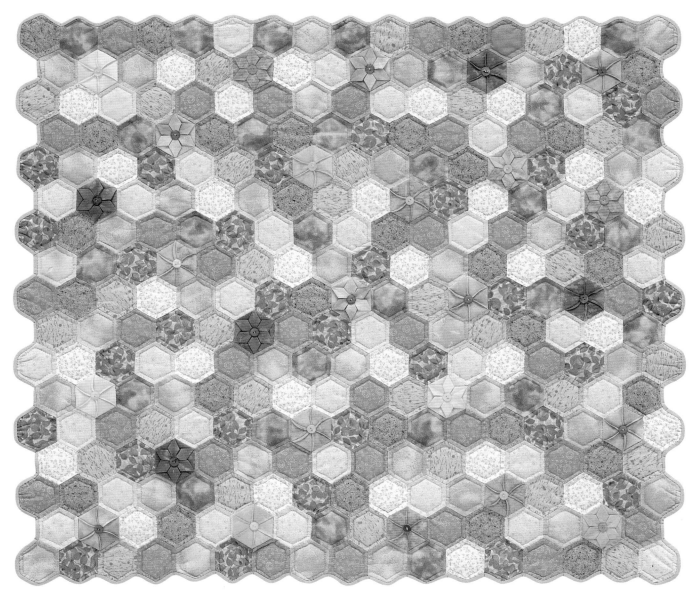

My Flower Garden, 43" x 39¹/₂", Rebecca Wat, quilted by Virginia Dunlap

The traditional pattern, Grandmother's Flower Garden, was adapted for *My Flower Garden*. Three-dimensional hexagon flowers add color, dimension, and interest to this quilt design. Since these three-dimensional hexagons are regular hexagons like any other hexagon in this quilt, they fit together naturally. Two three-dimensional hexagon designs were used in this quilt, curved-petal hexagon and diamond-petal hexagon, which are both fun and easy to make. Please note that this project is designed for hand piecing only.

Materials

Folded Hexagon Flowers: a variety to total 1 yard

Green Hexagons: a variety to total 2²/₃ yards

Binding: ²/₃ yard fabric to make your own bias, or 6¹/₂ yards of purchased pre-made single fold bias tape

Backing: 1¹/₃ yards

Batting: 44" x 47"

Cutting

Folded Hexagon Flowers: Cut 24 hexagons from a variety of fabrics using the 3" Hexagon template pattern, page 90.

Hexagons: Cut 281 hexagons from a variety of green fabrics, using the Hexagon for Piecing template pattern, page 90.

Folding

Following the Folding Instructions, pages 59-61, make 24 three-dimensional hexagon flowers using both the curved-petal and diamond-petal variations.

Construction

1. Mark the back of each green hexagon with six dots as shown on the Hexagon for Piecing template pattern, page 90. These dots provide guidelines for a ¹/₄" seam allowance. Sew the hexagons together by hand.

2. Another alternative is the English paper-piecing method:

Cut a number of hexagons out of paper (use the Hexagon for Piecing template pattern, page 90, without the seam allowance). The paper can be reused so you do not have to cut enough for all the hexagons.

Place the paper in the center of a hexagon that has been cut from fabric or use paper as a template to cut fabric, adding ¹/₄" seam allowance.

Turn the seam allowances over the edges of the paper and baste through the fabric and paper. Make sure the basting stitches can be easily removed. Prepare enough of these hexagons to sew a row or section of the quilt.

To sew, place two hexagon edges together and use a small stitch to join the two sides to each other. Be sure to start and stop exactly in the corners and secure your starting and ending stitches.

Remove the basting stitches and paper. The paper pieces can be reused.

3. Randomly appliqué the 24 folded hexagon flowers onto the quilt top.

4. Refer to pages 86-88 for general quilting and finishing instructions.

A Vest of Hexagons

A Vest of Hexagons, Rebecca Wat

I have always wanted a neutral colored vest that I could wear everyday, and yet be unique enough that I would not see its look-a-like everywhere on the street. The solution is this vest that satisfies all my requirements.

Materials

A simple commercial pattern for a loose-fitting vest

About half the amount of fabric indicated on the pattern (for the back of the vest only)

$1/2$ yard to make binding. If you prefer, purchase pre-made bias binding. Measure your vest pattern to determine how much bias binding you need.

Amount of lining and thin batting indicated on the pattern

Hexagons: $1/4$ yard each of four coordinating fabrics. (One fabric can be the same as the vest back and binding if you like.)

Folded Hexagons: $1/2$ yard

Number of buttons indicated on the pattern plus 8 buttons for the Folded Hexagons

3" Hexagon and Hexagon for Piecing template patterns, page 90.

Cutting

Pattern Preparation: Choose the right size from the pattern. Consider using the next larger size since heavy quilting will reduce the size of the finished garment. Cut on the stitching line of the correct size, adding $5/8$" to side and shoulder seams. If you prefer, trace the **stitching line** of your size on tracing paper, adding $5/8$" seam allowances at the side and shoulder seams. Then cut the pattern from the tracing paper.

Vest: Cut the back from a single piece of fabric. Using the pattern as a guide, cut the vest fronts and back from the lining and batting.

Hexagons: Using the Hexagon for Piecing template pattern, cut about 80 hexagons from vest and coordinating fabrics. Adjust the number of hexagons for your size and style of vest. Using the 3" Hexagon template pattern, cut 8 hexagons from vest, or coordinating fabrics for the folded hexagons

Folding

Fold and finger-press the eight 3-D hexagons following the steps shown in the Folding Instructions, pages 60-61.

Construction

1. Sew the hexagons together by hand, making two pieces large enough to cover both sides of the vest front. See page 66 for two different sewing methods.

2. Using the pattern as a guide, cut out the front from the pieces created in the previous step.

3. Appliqué the 3-D folded hexagons onto the vest.

4. Pin or baste the three layers (vest front and back, batting, and lining) together.

5. Quilt $1/4$" away from the seams, or as desired.

6. Using a $5/8$" seam allowance and shorter stitch length, sew the shoulder seams and side seams right-sides together.

7. Cut excess seam allowances from shoulder seams and side seams, leaving no more than $1/4$" remaining. Press. Cover raw edges with bias binding and blind stitch in place as shown on page 89.

8. Pin and sew binding onto the vest fabric. Then turn the binding over the raw edges of the vest. Blind stitch onto the lining side.

9. Make buttonholes and sew on buttons.

Hexagon Pillow

Hexagon Pillow, Rebecca Wat

$\mathcal{E}$ven those with very little sewing experience can make a hexagon pillow. A handful of pillows can be put together in a couple of hours with a hexagon cut for the desired size. Like the *Pinwheel Pillow*, the *Hexagon Pillow* is unique and certain to attract attention.

Materials

Use the hexagon pattern made in Steps 1-5 to determine the amount of fabric required.

One covered-button

Polyester filling

Construction

1. To create a hexagon pattern the size you want, cut a square that is twice as large as you want the finished pillow. Fold the square in half.

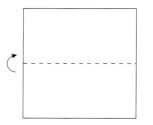

2. Fold the rectangle into fourths. Finger-press the folds and then open the rectangle.

3. From the folded edge place a bottom corner to touch the farthest crease line, creating a diagonal fold from the centerline of the rectangle. Finger-press the diagonal fold. Open the rectangle and repeat for the other bottom corner. Finger-press the diagonal fold. Note that you will also have the diagonal crease line of the previous fold as a guide.

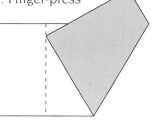

4. Fold the rectangle along the diagonal crease lines. Draw a horizontal line. Then cut along the drawn line "a" ("a" is the desired length of the sides of the hexagon.)

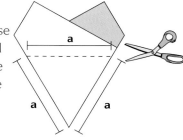

5. Open the triangle.

6. Piece fabrics together as needed and cut a hexagon using the pattern formed in Step 5.

7. Align the hexagon following the steps shown in Folding Instructions, Diamond-Petal Hexagon, pages 60-61.

8. Stuff the pillow with polyester filling.

9. Stitch to secure the center. Sew on the covered button.

Polygon Flower Garden

Polygon Flower Garden, 42" x 21", Rebecca Wat

$\mathcal{P}$entagon and octagon flowers are two types of polygon flowers used in this pictorial wallhanging. There are two basic design elements in this quilt: first, tall angular pieces of background fabric contrast the curves of the stems and leaves; second, the colorful flowers are placed against the brown, green, and white background.

Materials

Folded Pentagon Flowers: $^1/_3$ yard

Folded Octagon Flowers: $^1/_4$ yard

Background (white): $^1/_2$ yard

Background, Stems, and Leaves: a variety of greens and browns to total $^1/_2$ yard

Border and Binding: $1^1/_4$ yards

Buttons: 19 round buttons with holes in the centers 3 decorative ladybug buttons (optional)

Backing: $1^1/_4$ yards (If fabric is wider than 42", then $^3/_4$ yard is enough.)

Batting: 25" x 46"

$3^1/_4$ " Pentagon template pattern, page 91

$2^1/_2$ " Octagon template pattern, page 91

Leaf for Polygon Flower Garden template pattern, page 90

Cutting

Folded Pentagons: Use $3^1/_4$" Pentagon template pattern to trace and cut 13 pentagons.

Folded Octagons: Use $2^1/_2$" Octagon template pattern to trace and cut 6 octagons.

Stems: Cut 1"-wide bias strips of green fabric. You will need 2 yards in length.

Leaves: Use Leaf for Polygon Flower Garden template pattern to cut 6 leaves from various green fabrics. If you want to appliqué the leaves by hand, add a $^3/_{16}$" seam allowance around the pattern. Note: If you choose to make pieced leaves, add $^1/_4$" seam allowance along the centerline of both halves of the leaf pattern.

To make the quilt as shown, cut the green, brown, and white background fabrics according to the diagram below. But feel free to cut strips and triangles in different shapes and sizes. Fabric can be cut with seam allowances for piecing, or hand appliqué; or greens and browns can be cut to exact size for machine appliqué.

Borders and Binding: Refer to page 85 for help cutting correct lengths, if needed.
◆ Borders: Cut four 4¹/₂"-wide strips lengthwise.
◆ Binding: Cut four 3¹/₄"-wide strips lengthwise. Refer to pages 87-88 to make binding.

Folding

Fold and finger-press the 13 pentagons and 6 octagons following steps shown in the Folding Instructions, pages 61-63. You can either sew the buttons on at this point or as you hand appliqué the flowers.

Construction

1. Piece the strips and tall triangles together, similar to a crazy quilt, to create the background. If you have never pieced a crazy quilt before, practice piecing some irregular strips and triangles together. Or you can appliqué the green and brown triangles onto the white background. Press.

2. Trim the edges to form a rectangle the size you want. The quilt pictured is cut 13¹/₂" x 34¹/₂".

3. For the stems, stitch bias strips wrong-sides together lengthwise using an ¹/₈" seam allowance. Press the seam open on the back side. You can use a bias bar to press the bias strips. Cut stems to desired lengths.

4. If you are making leaves from two different fabrics, sew them together. Press seam open and trim if needed. Pin the appliqué leaves and stems in position, and baste before you appliqué them onto the background.

5. Arrange the flowers randomly over the background; pin and stitch them in place.

6. Add the mitered borders. Refer to pages 85-86 for further instructions, if needed. Press seams toward borders.

7. Refer to pages 86-88 for general quilting and finishing instructions.

Background layout

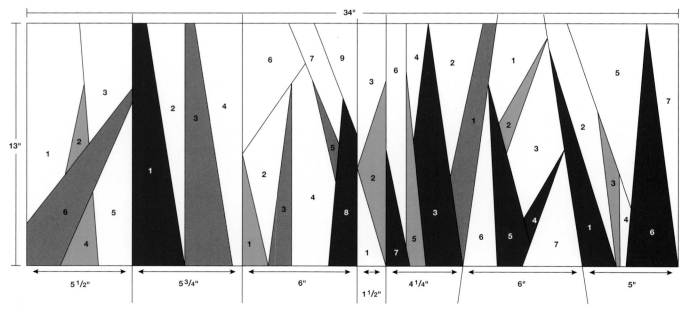

Note: Numbers indicate sewing order within each section. Dimensions are finished sizes, add seam allowances.

What's the Name of That Flower?

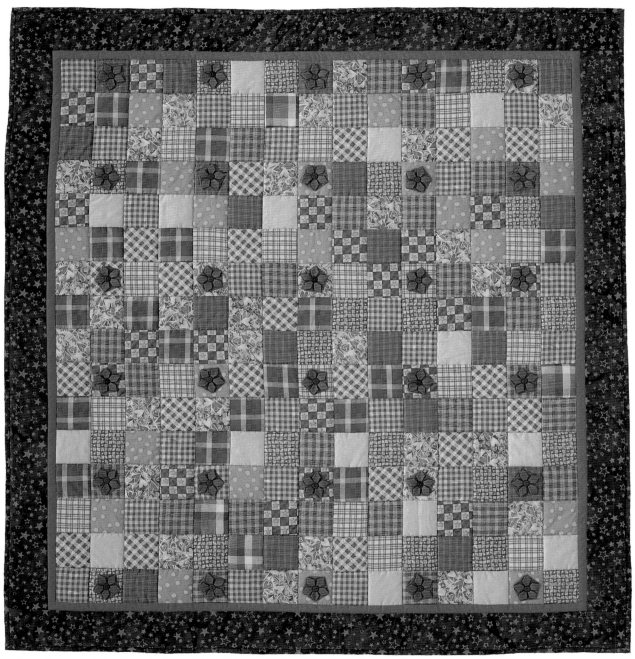

What's the Name of That Flower?, 63" x 66½", Rebecca Wat, quilted by Julie Murphy

This quilt is my tribute to a place called childhood where imagination has no boundaries and fun never ceases. The quilt uses approximately fifteen colorful fabrics to create a playful background on which three-dimensional pentagon flowers grow. There is no reason why you cannot use other polygon flowers or a combination of different flowers as appliqués. In any case, be prepared to answer the question: *What's the name of that flower?*

Materials

Background: A colorful variety to total 3 yards
Folded Pentagons: 1 yard
Inner Border: $^1/_3$ yard
Outer Border and Binding: 2 yards
Backing: 4 yards
Batting: 67" x 71"
Buttons: 30 round buttons with holes in the center
$3^1/_4$" Pentagon template pattern, page 91

Cutting

Pentagons: Cut 30 using $3^1/_4$" Pentagon template pattern.

Background: Cut two hundred forty 4" squares from various colorful fabrics. An alternative is to cut 4"-wide strips and piece them together randomly, then cut them into 4"-wide units.

Borders and Binding: Refer to page 85 for help cutting correct lengths, if needed.
◆ Inner Border: Cut seven $1^1/_2$"-wide strips crosswise. (Piece strips together end-to-end. Then cut to required lengths.)
◆ Outer Border: Cut four $4^1/_2$"-wide strips lengthwise.
◆ Binding: Cut four $3^1/_4$"-wide strips lengthwise. Refer to pages 87-88 to make binding.

Folding

Fold and finger-press the pentagons following steps shown in the Folding Instructions, pages 61-62. You can either sew the buttons on at this point or as you hand appliqué the flowers.

Construction

1. Arrange the squares, or blocks of squares, on a flat surface. Sew the squares together into rows. Press the seam allowances of each row in an alternate direction. (The alternately pressed seam allowances of the blocks should make matching the seams easier.)

2. Join the rows together matching seams. Press seams in one direction.

3. Place the flowers over the background as desired, then pin and appliqué them in place.

4. Add the side inner borders first, then the top and bottom inner borders. Press seams toward the border. Repeat for the outer border.

5. Refer to pages 86-88 for general quilting and finishing instructions.

More Sunflowers

More Sunflowers, 36¹/₂" x 40¹/₂", Rebecca Wat

Sunflowers are always popular. You may recall seeing fabrics with images of sunflowers and many other sunflower quilt designs, too. Sunflowers are so great that you never tire of looking at them. How about making a quilt with three-dimensional sunflowers? Since this quilt is made of a number of blocks, each with a different design, you can choose individual blocks to make a smaller quilt or a pillow. Although the sunflower seems to be the most challenging origami design presented in this chapter, the fabric folding technique required remains the same. Once you know how to make any of the flowers, you will have no problem creating this folded shape.

Materials

Folded Sunflowers: 1/2 yard
Sunflower Centers: 1/8 yard
Stems and Leaves: 3/8 yard
Background: 1/4 yard each of six fabrics
Sashing: 1/2 yard
Inner Border: 1/4 yard
Outer Border and Binding: 1 1/4 yards
Backing: 1 1/4 yards
Batting: 41" x 45"
12-Sided Polygon and Sunflower Center template patterns, page 92
Leaf A, B C template patterns, page 93

Cutting

Folded Sunflowers: Cut 9 using 12-Sided Polygon template pattern.

Sunflower Centers: Cut 9 using Sunflower Center template patterns.

Background:
◆ Cut one 8 1/2" square (block A)
◆ Cut one 8 1/2" x 12 1/2" rectangle (block C)
◆ Cut one 6 1/2" x 15 1/2" rectangle (block G)
◆ Cut one 8 1/2" x 7 1/2" rectangle (block D)
◆ Cut one 8 1/2" x 6 1/2" rectangle (block F)
◆ Cut one 5 1/2" x 16 1/2" rectangle (block J)

Sashing:
◆ Cut two 2 1/2" x 8 1/2" strips (B and E)
◆ Cut one 2 1/2" x 15 1/2" strip (H)
◆ Cut one 2 1/2" x 16 1/2" strip (I)
◆ Cut one 2 1/2" x 22 1/2" strip (K)
◆ Cut four 2 1/2" x 26 1/2" strips (L,M,N,O)

Stems: Cut 1"-wide bias strips. You will need approximately 1 yard in length.

Leaves: If you wish to appliqué the leaves by hand, add a 3/16" seam allowance around the pattern.
Note: If you choose to make pieced leaves, add a 1/4" seam allowance along the centerline of both halves of the leaf pattern.
◆ Cut 3 using Leaf A template pattern.
◆ Cut 2 using Leaf B template pattern.
◆ Cut 2 using Leaf C template pattern.

Borders and Binding: Refer to page 85 for cutting correct lengths, if needed.
◆ Inner Border: Cut four 1 1/2"-wide strips.
◆ Outer Border: Cut four 4 1/2"-wide strips lengthwise.
◆ Binding: Cut four 3 1/4"strips lengthwise. Refer to pages 87-88 to make binding.

Folding

Fold and finger-press the sunflowers following steps shown in the Folding Instructions, page 64.

Construction

1. Appliqué the sunflower centers to the sunflowers by hand or machine.

2. For the stems, stitch bias strips wrong-sides together lengthwise using an 1/8" seam allowance. Press seam open on back side. You can use a bias bar to press the bias strips. Cut stems to desired lengths. Pin, baste, and appliqué stems in place.

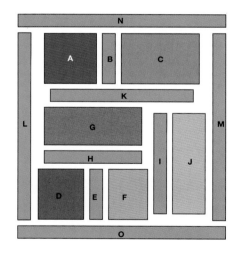

3. Add the sashing strips to the background blocks.

4. Sew leaves together if making pieced leaves. Press seams open. Trim if needed. Pin, baste, and appliqué the leaves in place by hand or machine.

5. Pin and appliqué the sunflowers in place.

6. Add the side inner borders first, then the top and bottom inner borders. Press seams toward the border. To add the outer mitered borders, refer to pages 85-86, if needed. Press seams toward the outer border.

7. Refer to pages 86-88 for general quilting and finishing instructions.

Kimonos

*K*imonos are known for their unique form of beauty and style. The use of layers of exquisite fabrics in a kimono enhances its beauty and elegance, as well as indicates the cultural richness of the country the kimono represents. If you want to make a quilt that has a strong Oriental essence, or if you want to showcase your proud collection of Oriental inspired fabrics, you will find the kimono designs in this chapter very helpful.

Two different designs are introduced here, which show both the front and back views of a kimono. The designs are adaptations of the T-block pattern, on which waistbands and collars are added to achieve a three-dimensional effect. I found the most enjoyable part of making the kimono blocks is that I was able to mix and match many wonderful, but rarely-used, Oriental inspired fabrics. These unique patterns and color combinations, along with the three-dimensional designs, make the kimonos lively.

The Bow

1. With the fabric wrong-side up, fold in ¹/₄" on all four sides. Iron-press the folds.

2. Turn the fabric right-side up. Make even width pleats and finger-press them.

3. Gather and stitch pleats together in the middle to form a bow (View A).

4. Draw the lower corners of the bow together to form a fan shape (View B). Stitch the two sides together at the back.

The Front Collar

5. With the fabric wrong-side up, fold in ¹/₄ of the width from the top and bottom raw edges. Iron-press.

Then fold the piece in half so that the raw edges are hidden inside. Iron-press.

6. Bend the two sides toward the center. Iron-press.

The Back Collar

7. With the fabric wrong-side up, fold in ¹/₄" from all four sides. Iron-press.

The Waistband

8. With the fabric wrong-side up, fold in ¹/₄" from all four sides. Iron-press.

Kimono - Front View

9. After piecing the block, pin the collar in place, overlapping ends. Hand stitch to secure the inside neck and the outside (lapel) edges of the collar.

10. Pin and hand stitch the waistband in position, covering raw edges of the collar.

Kimono - Back View

11. View A—Bow style: Pin and hand stitch the back collar and waistband in place. Pin the bow on top of the band and hand stitch in place. For greater washability, secure around the bow.

12. View B—Fan style: Pin and stitch the back collar and waistband in place. Place the bow on top of the band and stitch in place. This is an option to View A, created by stitching the edges of the bow together. For greater washability, secure around the fan.

Kimono Sampler II, 57½ " x 57½", Rebecca Wat

Sixteen kimonos are showcased in *Kimono Sampler* I. The kimonos are arranged so that four are grouped together in each corner. There are many alternate ways to arrange the kimono blocks. Have fun arranging the blocks in different ways and exploring many possibilities before sewing them together.

Materials

Kimonos: 1/3 yard each of four fabrics

Waistbands, Bows, and Collars: 1/4 yard each of four fabrics

Background (white): 1 1/2 yards

Inner Border: 1/4 yard

Outer Border and Binding: 1 3/4 yards

Backing: 3 1/2 yards

Batting: 62" x 62"

Cutting

Kimonos: Cut two 4³/₄"-wide strips of each fabric. Then cut four 4³/₄" squares (B), and four 4³/₄" x 13¹/₄" rectangles (E) from each pair of strips. You will need 16 squares (B) and 16 rectangles (E) total.

Bows, Waistbands, and Collars:

◆ Bows: Cut one 4³/₄"-wide strip of each fabric, then cut two 4³/₄" x 5" rectangles from each strip. You will need 8 rectangles total.

◆ Waistbands: Cut one 2"-wide strip of each fabric, then cut four 2" x 4³/₄" rectangles from each strip. You will need 16 rectangles total.

◆ Front Collars: Cut two 2" x 9" rectangles from each fabric. You will need 8 rectangles total.

◆ Back Collars: Cut two 1" x 3" rectangles from each fabric. You will need 8 rectangles total.

Background:

◆ For C and D: Cut two 7¹/₄"-wide strips, then cut strips into eight 7¹/₄" squares. Cut the squares diagonally twice. You will need 32 triangles.

◆ For A, F, and G: Cut three 3⁷/₈"-wide strips, then cut strips into twenty-four 3⁷/₈" squares. Cut the squares in half diagonally. You will need 48 triangles.

◆ For H: Cut two 9⁷/₈"-wide strips, then cut strips into eight 9⁷/₈" squares. Cut the squares in half diagonally. You will need 16 triangles.

Borders and Binding: Refer to page 85 for help cutting correct lengths, if needed.

◆ Inner Border: Cut six 1"-wide strips crosswise.

◆ Outer Border: Cut four 4¹/₂"-wide strips lengthwise.

◆ Binding: Cut four 3¹/₄"-wide strips lengthwise. Refer to pages 87-88 to make binding.

Folding

Make 8 bows, 8 front collars, 8 back collars, and 16 waistbands following steps shown in Folding Instructions, pages 76-77.

Construction

1. Assemble the kimono blocks, as shown. Measure and trim the block to 12¹/₂" square, if necessary.

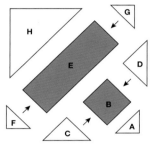

Block construction

2. Appliqué the front collars to 8 kimonos (front view).

3. Arrange and appliqué the 16 waistbands to each kimono.

4. Appliqué the back collars and bows to the 8 kimonos (back view).

5. Arrange the 16 blocks as shown or as desired. Sew them together in rows. Press seams of each row in an alternate direction. This makes matching seams easier.

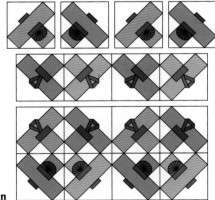

Quilt construction

6. Join the rows together. Press seams in one direction.

7. Add the inner side borders first, then the top and bottom inner borders. Press seams toward the border. Repeat for the outer border.

8. Refer to pages 86-88 for general quilting and finishing instructions.

Kimono Sampler II, 37¹/₂ " x 47 ", Rebecca Wat

The kimono blocks in *Kimono Sampler* II are different from that of the *Kimono Sampler* I in that they are "on point." Each is framed with four corner triangles and sashings. This arrangement highlights the individual kimonos. Using the same basic arrangement, it is very easy to convert the quilt to accommodate any number of kimonos you wish to display.

Materials

Kimonos: $^1/_8$ yard each of three fabrics

Waistbands, Bows, and Collars: scraps or $^1/_8$ yard each of three solid fabrics

Background (white): $^1/_2$ yard

Corner Triangles (gold): $^1/_2$ yard

Sashing: $^5/_8$ yard

Sashing Posts: $^1/_8$ yard

Border and Binding: $1^3/_8$ yards

Backing: $1^3/_8$ yards

Batting: 42" x 51"

Cutting

Kimonos:

◆ Cut four $2^1/_2$" squares (B) of each fabric.

◆ Cut four $2^1/_2$" x $6^1/_2$" rectangles (E) of each fabric.

Bows, Waistbands, and Collars:

◆ Bows: Cut two $2^1/_2$" x $2^3/_4$" rectangles of each fabric. You will need 6 rectangles total.

Waistbands: Cut four $1^1/_2$" x $2^1/_2$" rectangles of each fabric. You will need 12 rectangles total.

◆ Front Collars: Cut two $1^1/_2$" x 5" rectangles of each fabric. You will need 6 rectangles total.

◆ Back Collars: Cut two $^7/_8$" x $1^1/_2$" rectangles of each fabric. You will need 6 rectangles total.

Background:

◆ For A, F and G: cut one $2^1/_4$"-wide strip, then cut strip into eighteen $2^1/_4$" squares. Cut the squares in half diagonally. You will need 36 triangles.

◆ For C and D: cut one $4^1/_8$"-wide strip, then cut strip into six $4^1/_8$" squares. Cut the squares diagonally twice. You will need 24 triangles.

◆ For H, cut one $5^1/_8$"-wide strip, then cut strip into six $5^1/_8$" squares. Cut the squares in half diagonally. You will need 12 triangles.

Corner Triangles (Gold):

Cut three $4^7/_8$"-wide strips, then cut strips into twenty-four $4^7/_8$" squares. Cut squares in half diagonally. You will need 48 triangles.

Sashing:

Cut eight 2"-wide strips, then cut strip into 2" x $8^1/_2$" rectangles. You will need 31 rectangles.

Sashing Posts:

Cut one 2"-wide strip, then cut strip into 2" squares. You will need 20 squares.

Border and Binding:

Refer to page 85 for help cutting correct lengths, if needed.

◆ Border: Cut four 4"-wide strips lengthwise.

◆ Binding: Cut four $3^1/_4$" strips lengthwise. Refer to pages 87-88 to make binding.

Folding

Make 6 bows, 6 front collars, 6 back collars, and 12 waistbands following steps shown in Folding Instructions, pages 76-77.

Construction

1. Assemble the kimono blocks, as shown. Press. Measure and trim blocks to $6^1/_8$" square, if necessary.

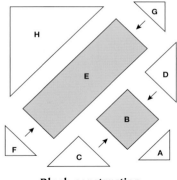

Block construction

2. Sew corner triangles to Kimono blocks as shown. Press seams toward corner triangles.

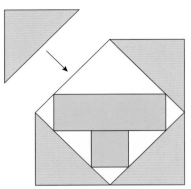

Adding corners to Kimono block

3. Appliqué the front collars to 6 kimonos (front view).

4. Appliqué in place the 12 waistbands to each kimono.

5. Appliqué the back collars and the bows to the 6 kimonos (back view).

6. Arrange the 12 blocks as desired. Sew the vertical sashing strips to three blocks to make a row. Press seams toward the sashing. Repeat this step three more times.

7. Sew four 2" posts to three sashing strips to form a horizontal sashing, as shown. Press seams toward the sashing. Repeat this step four more times.

8. Join rows of the horizontal sashings and blocks, as shown. Press toward the sashing.

9. Add the side borders first, then the top and bottom borders. Press seams toward the border.

10. Refer to pages 86-88 for general quilting and finishing instructions.

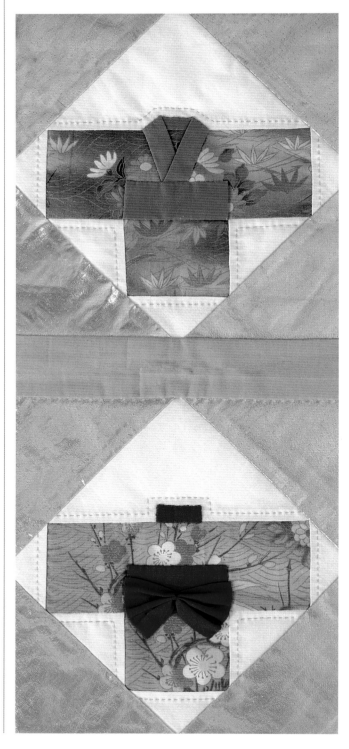

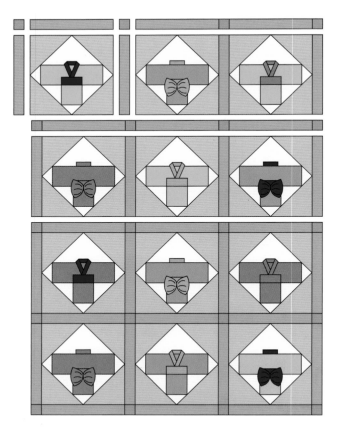

Quilt construction

Construction Techniques

There are many ways to make a quilt. The methods and techniques that quilters use to construct their quilts vary depending on their background, habits, personal style and preference. I learned quilting through reading extensively, watching tapes and TV shows, and making frequent visits to a local quilt shop where knowledgeable quilters were available to answer questions and share their opinions and experiences. Another effective way to learn is to attend classes. I encourage you to do all of the above if you love to quilt and want to improve your skills.

To serve as a simple reference for beginning quilters, I have simplified and divided the process of quiltmaking into the following topics.

Design/Preparation

It is helpful, if not vital, to have at least a general idea of the look and size of the quilt you intend to make. Sketch the design on a piece of paper. After refining the it, write down the measurements. Finalize the design and draw it on a piece of graph paper in the right proportions. Make a few copies so you can color each copy differently. Estimate the number of different fabrics you need and the yardage for each fabric, before heading to your favorite fabric store. Once you have assembled all the fabrics, plan a cutting scheme similar to the cutting instructions in this book. If you have a design to follow, ignore this design step.

Rotary Cutting

A rotary cutter, a cutting mat, and a wide acrylic ruler are essential for efficient and accurate cutting. If you have never used a rotary cutter before, have someone show you the proper way to use it. Before cutting, press the fabrics with an iron. Align the fabric with the horizontal markings on the mat, and the ruler with the vertical markings on the mat. Press down firmly on the ruler with four of your five fingertips. Your little finger should be against the outside edge of the ruler and resting on the mat or fabric to keep the ruler from shifting. Holding the cutter with the other hand, cut along the edge of the ruler (the blade of the cutter should

rotate during this process). Practice cutting scrap fabrics first. Do not cut the fabrics you will use until you have mastered the skill of rotary cutting. To cut multiple layers of fabric, be sure the folded edges align with the horizontal markings on the mat.

Rotary Cutting

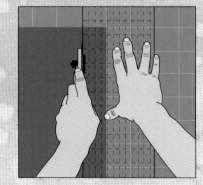

Left handed cutting

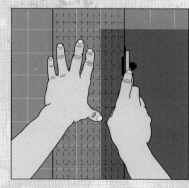

Right handed cutting

Piecing

Piecing can be done either by hand or machine. Regardless of the way you choose to piece, it is important to use a consistent seam allowance. To piece by hand, draw lines $1/4$" from the raw edges on the wrong side of the fabric with a marking tool. Place two pieces of fabric right-sides together, piece them together with very small running stitches and end by backstitching. When piecing by machine, there are several ways to sew $1/4$" seams:

1. Use a $1/4$" presser foot, generally available for most sewing machines. It is a good investment if you do much piecing.

2. If your machine sews zigzag, you may adjust the needle so that it is ¼" from the edge of the presser foot.

3. Find the ¼" mark on the throat plate next to the feed dogs of your machine and use a piece of tape to mark and extend it so you can use it for reference when you sew.

To piece more efficiently, arrange and sew the pieces in pairs, one after another, without cutting the thread or lifting the presser foot of the sewing machine. This is called chain piecing.

In most cases, you should press the seams toward the darker fabric. If possible, it is helpful to press the seams of rows of blocks in alternate directions to reduce the bulk at seams when the rows are joined to other rows. Some quilters prefer pressing the seams open. In any case, be sure you press the seams properly with an iron.

Chain piecing

Appliqués

There are many methods for appliqué. Most involve cutting templates from plastic, cardboard, or freezer paper. Appliqués can be sewn onto the background fabric either by hand or machine. To hand appliqué, add a seam allowance (approximately ³/₁₆") when cutting the appliqué shapes. The seam allowance can be turned under before or after you baste or pin the appliqué onto the background fabric. To machine appliqué, cut on the drawn lines of the appliqué. Baste or pin the appliqué shapes onto the background fabric before you begin satin stitching (a very close zigzag stitch) with your machine. When satin stitching, be sure the stitches are covering the raw edge of the appliqué, not the background fabric, and that all the corners and points of the appliqué are well covered.

Hand appliqué

Machine appliqué

Embroidery and Embellishments

Often times, embellishments on quilt tops can enhance the beauty of the quilt and add interest, as shown in many projects in this book. Buttons, beads, ribbons, yarn, and embroidery floss can be used for this decorative purpose. It is easier to add the embroidery and embellishments before assembling the blocks. However, in some cases, the embroidery and embellishments are designed to overlap the sashing and borders to enhance depth and feeling of motion, once the sashing and borders are added.

Sashing and Borders

Sashing is the strips of fabrics that are used to join blocks together. Always sew the shorter sashing on first, resulting in rows of blocks. Press the seam allowances toward the sashing. Then join the rows together with strips of longer sashing. When sewing on the long sashing, mark the center of the sashing and the quilt, then match and pin them in position first. Be sure not to stretch the fabrics when sewing since this will cause the fabric to wrinkle or ripple.

Borders are the strips of fabrics used to frame the whole quilt top. You will get more accurate measurements for the length of the borders by measuring through the center of the quilt top. As with attaching long horizontal sashing, mark the centers of the border and the quilt, then match and pin them in position before sewing. Do not stretch the fabric. Accurate and consistent seam allowances and frequent proper pressing are the keys to success in this step.

Two types of borders were used through out the projects in this book: straight borders and mitered borders. My way of sewing the mitered borders is slightly different from what most quilters do. I found that by folding under the corners and hand stitching them in place, greater accuracy and different degrees of angles are achieved easily.

Adding Straight Borders

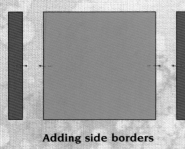

Adding side borders

Adding top and bottom borders

Adding Mitered Borders

(1) Mark and match centers. Pin and sew two borders to the quilt top, right-sides together, across from each other.

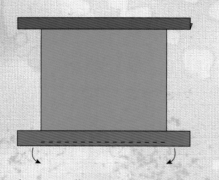

Press the seam allowances toward the border.

(2) Mark and match centers. Pin and sew the other two borders to the quilt top, right-sides together, beginning and ending exactly where they intersect the adjacent borders.

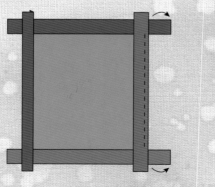

Press the seam allowances toward the border.

(3) Turn under the corners of the borders to form mitered corners. Press the folds, being careful not to stretch the fabric since the fold is on the bias.

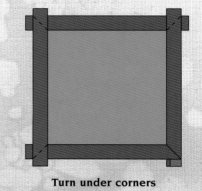

Turn under corners

(4) Pin and slip stitch the corners in place along the diagonal fold lines. Trim the excess fabric.

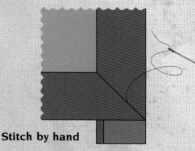

Stitch by hand

Marking

Mark the quilting designs onto the quilt top with your favorite marking tool. It is quite common for quilters to quilt $1/8$" to $1/4$" away from the seam line and around all appliqués. You may also choose to follow the prints on the fabric or to quilt as close to the seam line as possible, i.e. quilt-in-the-ditch, in which case there is no need to mark the quilt. There are also stencils for quilt marking available in craft stores and quilt shops.

Backing

For many quilts, you will need to sew fabrics together to make a large enough backing. Cut the selvages from the fabrics first—they tend to be stiff and woven more tightly so you don't want to use them. Determine a balanced layout of fabric, either with all pieces of equal size or with the larger piece of fabric in the center and pieces of equal size on either side. Backings can be pieced either horizontally or vertically. You can also make a patchwork backing by using fabric from the front of the quilt or fabrics that relate well to the front.

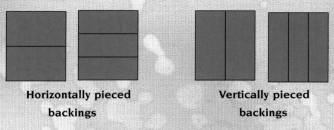

Horizontally pieced backings   **Vertically pieced backings**

Basting

A quilt is made of three layers: quilt top, batting, and backing fabric. It is important to baste the three layers together properly before quilting. Place the backing wrong-side up on a flat surface. Smooth the fabric and tape all corners and edges to the surface with masking tape. Spread the batting on top of the backing and place the quilt top on the top, smoothing all the wrinkles. Hold the layers together either with long running stitches or with safety pins. The most commonly used method is to baste or pin in a grid, with the intersections no more than 3" apart (see below). Trim the batting at least $\frac{1}{2}$" beyond the quilt top. Trim the backing so it extends 2" beyond the quilt top on all sides. Before quilting, you can wrap the extra backing fabric over the raw edges of the quilt to protect the edges from fraying.

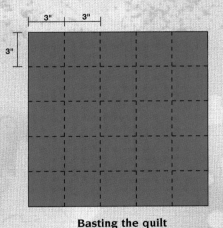

Basting the quilt

Quilting

Quilting can be done either by hand or machine. To quilt by hand, stitch through all the layers using small running stitches, beginning and ending the stitches with knots. Hide the knots in the batting layer by giving the thread a quick tug. To quilt by machine, take the time to test and find the settings for the right tension and stitch length. Use a walking foot made for quilting to help feed the fabrics evenly. Lay the quilt on a flat surface and roll the left, right, and bottom sides up toward the center, exposing a column of area to

quilt in the center. Roll and unroll the quilt as you go to expose a small area to be quilted. Always quilt from the center outward and quilt all areas in one direction before turning in another direction.

Sleeve

If you plan to hang the quilt, attach a sleeve before sewing the binding to the backing. To make a sleeve, cut an 8"-wide strip the width of the quilt. Turn under $\frac{1}{4}$" twice at each narrow end and sew. Fold the strip in half lengthwise and sew it to the back at the top of the quilt using no more than a $\frac{1}{4}$" seam allowance. This will make a $3\frac{3}{4}$"-wide sleeve. Slip or whip stitch the opposite long edge of the sleeve to the back of the quilt, being sure that the stitches do not show on the front of the quilt.

Binding

Use a rotary cutter and a wide ruler to trim off excess batting and backing from the quilt. Determine the length of the binding by adding up the measurements of the four sides plus a 12" allowance. To make a double-fold binding, multiply the desired finished width by six and add another $\frac{1}{4}$" to it, for instance, a $3\frac{1}{4}$"-wide strip will make a half-inch finished binding. For straight binding, cut fabric lengthwise or crosswise. To bind quilts with irregular edges, cut bias strips from the binding fabric. Regardless of whether the binding is cut on the straight grain or bias, the strips should be sewn together at a 45° angle to reduce the bulk once the binding is sewn to the quilt or garment.

Piecing binding strips at 45° angle

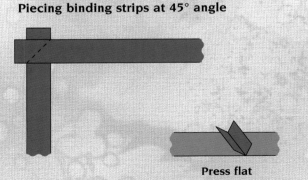

Press flat

There are two methods for making bias depending on the length strips needed and personal preference. You can cut strips on the bias and piece them together at a 45° angle to create strips of the needed length.
Some people prefer to make "continuous strip" bias. Refer to your favorite sewing book for instructions.

To bind the quilt, fold the binding strip in half lengthwise, wrong-sides together. Then align the raw edges of the binding strip with that of the quilt. Pin the strip in place. Before sewing the binding, you should lay the binding around the quilt to make sure that none of the binding seams will be on a corner.

Sewing on the binding.

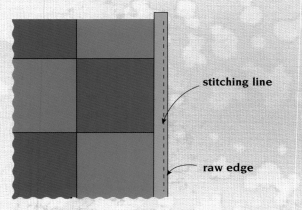

stitching line

raw edge

You have two options for the corners:

1. You can overlap the ends for a straight edge, called an overlapped corner. Stitch binding to opposite sides and trim even with the quilt. Add the top and bottom binding strips, trimming ½" beyond the edge. Fold binding over to cover the machine stitches and the corner's raw edge. Blind stitch to backing and secure corners.

2. Follow the directions below to make mitered corners.

Making Mitered Binding Corners

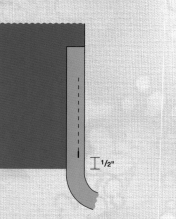

½"

(1) Start sewing in the middle of a side, leaving a few inches of binding free. For a ½"-wide finished binding; stop sewing exactly ½" away from the corner. Back stitch.

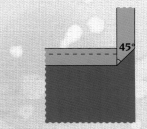

45°

(2) Turn the quilt counter-clockwise 90°. Fold the binding up, forming a 45° angle.

(3) Fold the binding down. Start stitching from top of the border. Repeat on the remaining corners.

Joining Ends of Binding

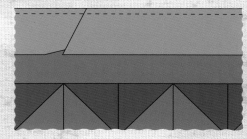

To join the ends of the binding, stop about 4" from where you want to join the ends. Remove the quilt from the sewing machine. Fold in the starting edge of the binding ¼" and slip the ending edge into it, trimming any excess. Stitch the final section of the binding to the quilt. Fold the binding over the raw edges and machine stitches. Blind stitch to backing, securing the corners and the end joint.

Labeling

Be sure to sign and date your work with a label on the back of the quilt. Labels can be plain or fancy, written with a permanent-marking pen or stitched by hand or machine.

Binding for Vests

When making quilted vests, trim the seam allowances to a scant ¼", press open, and cover with bias binding as shown. Make certain your bias binding is wide enough to cover the seam allowance. Blind stitch the binding in place, completely covering the raw edges of the seam allowances.

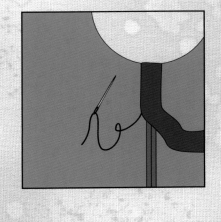

Template Patterns

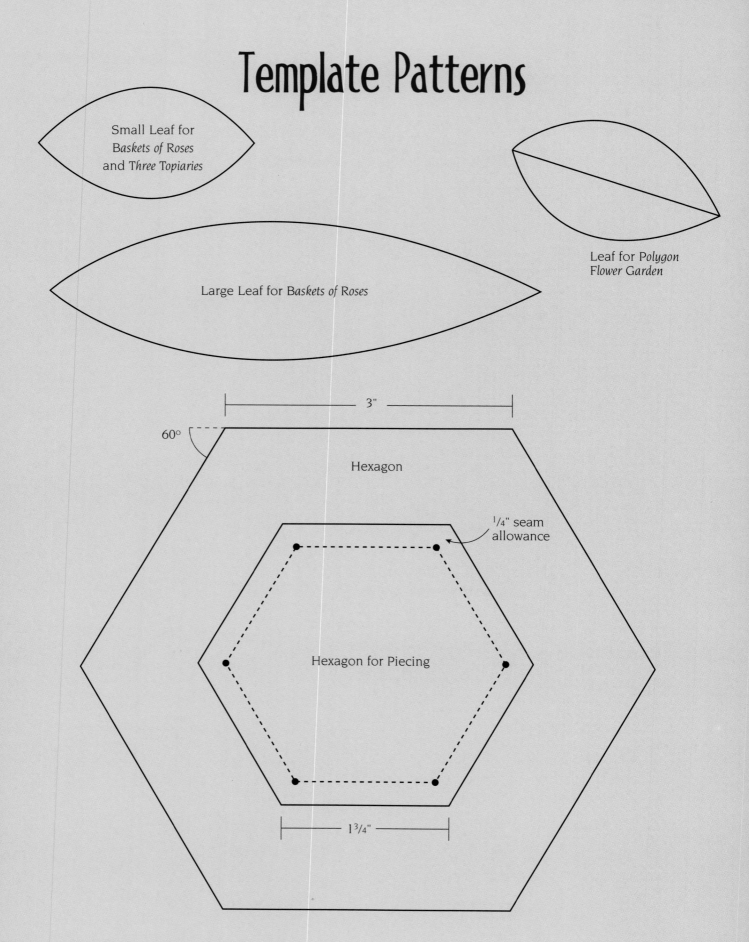

Small Leaf for *Baskets of Roses* and *Three Topiaries*

Leaf for *Polygon Flower Garden*

Large Leaf for *Baskets of Roses*

3"

60°

Hexagon

¼" seam allowance

Hexagon for Piecing

1³⁄₄"

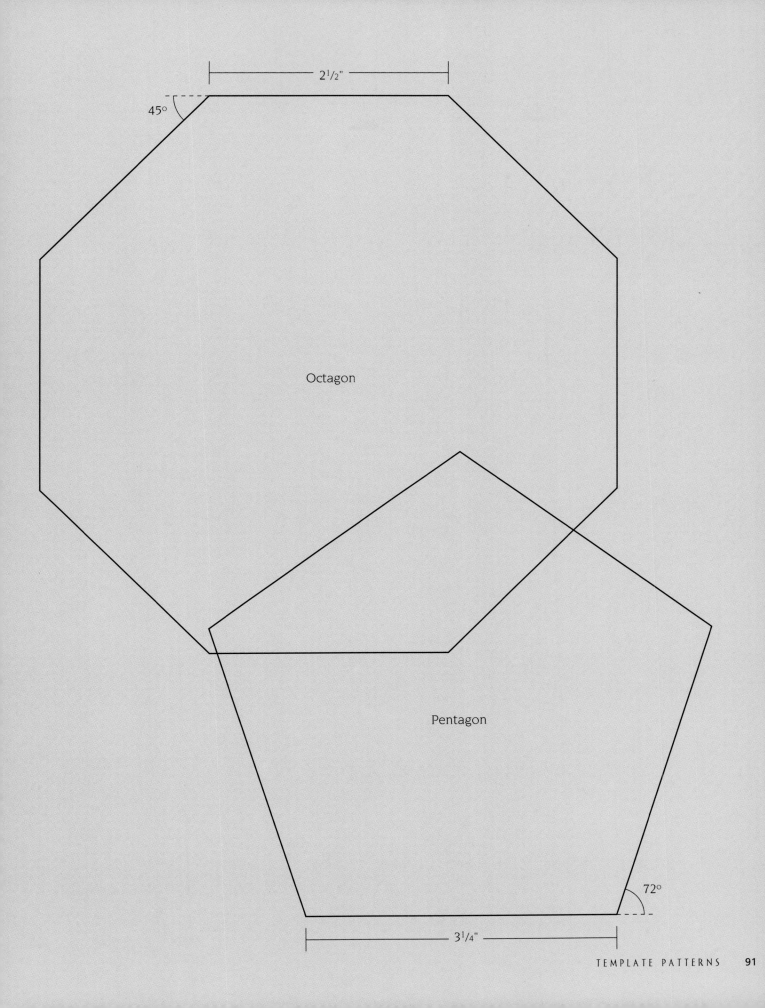

2¹/₂"

45°

Octagon

Pentagon

72°

3¹/₄"

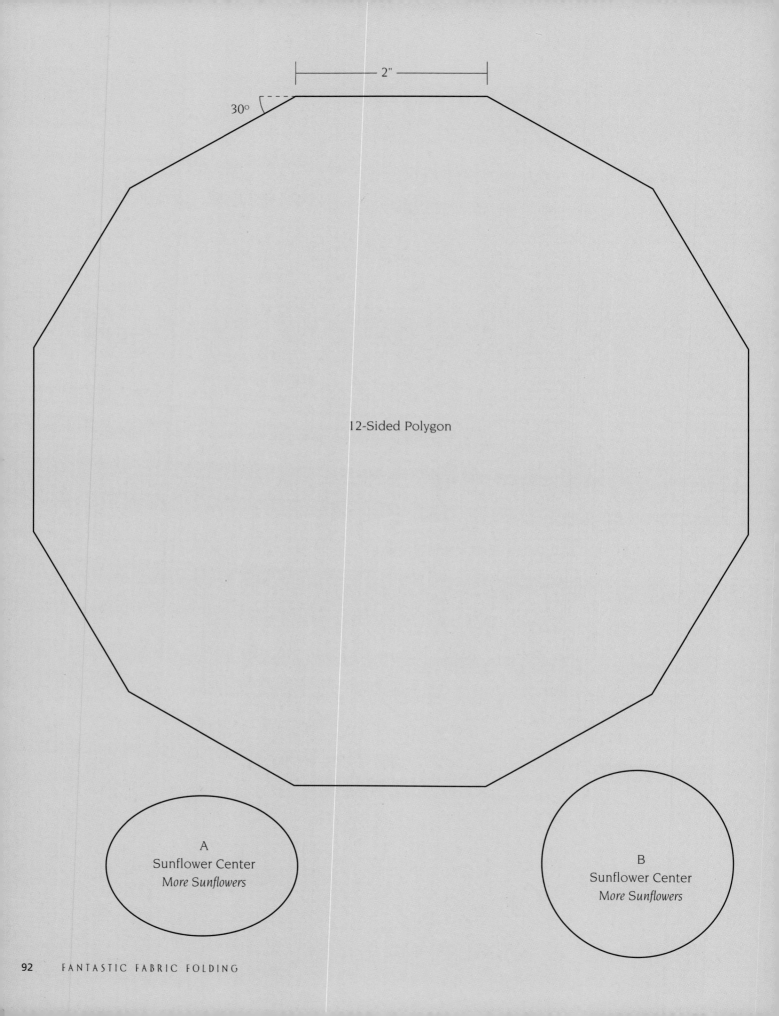

2"

30°

12-Sided Polygon

A
Sunflower Center
More Sunflowers

B
Sunflower Center
More Sunflowers

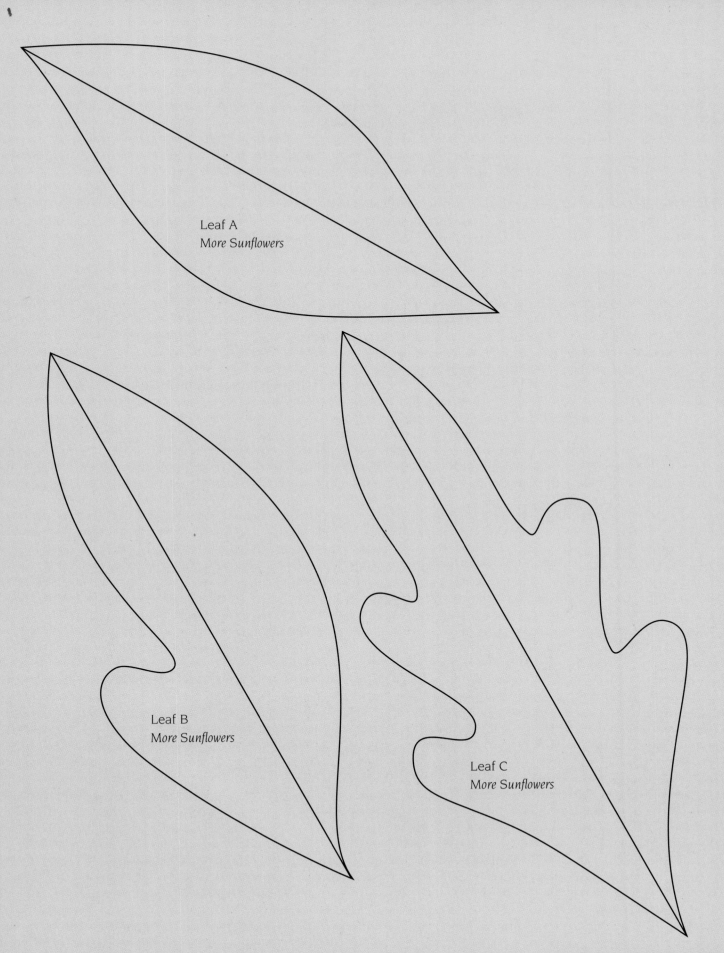

Leaf A
More Sunflowers

Leaf B
More Sunflowers

Leaf C
More Sunflowers

Index

About the Author

Rebecca Wat is an origami expert, a quiltmaker, and wearable-art designer. Her idea to apply origami techniques to quilting has resulted in the birth of a new kind of three-dimensional quilt. Her work has appeared in various international quilt shows and museums. Rebecca is currently committed to sharing her quilting experience and ideas through writing and teaching. She welcomes quilt lovers, crafters, and fiber-artists to visit her web site at www.3Dquilt.com.

Bibliography

Anderson, Alex. *Start Quilting with Alex Anderson* Lafayette, CA: C&T Publishing, Inc., 1997

Anderson, Alex. *Hand Quilting with Alex Anderson.* Lafayette, CA: C&T Publishing, Inc.,1998

Anderson, Alex. *Rotary Cutting with Alex Anderson.* Lafayette, CA: C&T Publishing, Inc., 1999

Fons, Marianne and Liz Porter. *Quilter's Complete Guide.* Oxmoor House, 1993

McClun, Diana and Laura Nownes. *Quilts! Quilts!! Quilts!!! The Complete Guide to Quiltmaking.* San Francisco: The Quilt Digest Press, 1988. Second ed., 1997

McClun, Diana and Laura Nownes. *Quilts, Quilts, and More Quilts!* Lafayette, CA: C&T Publishing, Inc. 1993

Other Fine Books From C&T Publishing:

15 Two-Block Quilts: Unlock the Secrets of Secondary Patterns, Claudia Olson

250 Continuous-Line Quilting Designs for Hand, Machine & Long-Arm Quilters, Laura Lee Fritz

All About Quilting from A to Z, From the Editors and Contributors of Quilter's Newsletter Magazine and Quiltmaker Magazine

America from the Heart: Quilters Remember September 11, 2001, Karey Bresenhan

Appliqué 12 Easy Ways!: Charming Quilts, Giftable Projects, & Timeless Techniques, Elly Sienkiewicz

Best of Baltimore Beauties Part II, The: More Patterns for Album Blocks, Elly Sienkiewicz

Block Magic: Over 50 Fun & Easy Blocks from Squares and Rectangles, Nancy Johnson-Srebro

Bouquet of Quilts, A: Garden-Inspired Projects for the Home, Edited by Jennifer Rounds & Cyndy Lyle Rymer

Butterflies & Blooms: Designs for Appliqué & Quilting, Carol Armstrong

Cats in Quilts: 14 Purrfect Projects, Carol Armstrong

Color from the Heart: Seven Great Ways to Make Quilts with Colors You Love, Gai Perry

Color Play: Easy Steps to Imaginative Color in Quilts, Joen Wolfrom

Cotton Candy Quilts: Using Feed Sacks, Vintage, and Reproduction Fabrics, Mary Mashuta

Cozy Cabin Quilts from Thimbleberries: 20 Projects for Any Home, Lynette Jensen

Create Your Own Quilt Labels!, Kim Churbuck

Cut-Loose Quilts: Stack, Slice, Switch, and Sew, Jan Mullen

Elm Creek Quilts: Quilt Projects Inspired by the Elm Creek Quilts Novels, Jennifer Chiaverini & Nancy Odom

Enchanted Views: Quilts Inspired by Wrought-Iron Designs, Dilys Fronks

Four Seasons in Flannel: 23 Projects—Quilts & More, Jean Wells & Lawry Thorn

Floral Stitches: An Illustrated Guide to Floral Stitchery, Judith Baker Montano

Free Stuff for Quilters on the Internet, 3rd Edition, Judy Heim & Gloria Hansen

Free-Style Quilts: A "No Rules" Approach, Susan Carlson

Garden-Inspired Quilts: Design Journals for 12 Quilt Projects, Jean & Valori Wells

Hand Quilting with Alex Anderson: Six Projects for First-Time Hand Quilters, Alex Anderson

Hidden Block Quilts: • Discover New Blocks Inside Traditional Favorites • 13 Quilt Settings • Instructions for 76 Blocks, Lerlene Nevaril

In the Nursery: Creative Quilts and Designer Touches, Jennifer Sampou & Carolyn Schmitz

Kids Start Quilting with Alex Anderson: •7 Fun & Easy Projects •Quilts for Kids by Kids •Tips for Quilting with Children, Alex Anderson

Laurel Burch Quilts: Kindred Creatures, Laurel Burch

Lone Star Quilts and Beyond: Step-by-Step Projects and Inspiration, Jan Krentz

Mastering Machine Appliqué, 2nd Edition: The Complete Guide Including: • Invisible Machine Appliqué • Satin Stitch • Blanket Stitch & Much More, Harriet Hargrave

Mastering Quilt Marking: Marking Tools and Techniques, Choosing Stencils, Matching Borders and Corners, Pepper Cory

Paper Piecing Picnic: Fun-Filled Projects for Every Quilter, From the Editors and Contributors of Quilter's Newsletter Magazine and Quiltmaker Magazine

Paper Piecing with Alex Anderson: •Tips •Techniques •6 Projects, Alex Anderson

Pieced Flowers, Ruth B. McDowell

Provence Quilts and Cuisine, Marie-Christine Flocard & Cosabeth Parriaud

Q is for Quilt, Diana McClun & Laura Nownes

Quick Quilts for the Holidays: 11 Projects to Stamp, Stencil, and Sew, Trice Boerens

Quilted Garden, The: Design & Make Nature-Inspired Quilts, Jane Sassaman

Quilting Back to Front: Fun & Easy No-Mark Techniques, Larraine Scouler

Quilts, Quilts, and More Quilts!, Diana McClun & Laura Nownes

Rag Wool Appliqué: •Easy to Sew •Use Any Sewing Machine •Quilts, Home Decor & Clothing, Kathy MacMannis

Setting Solutions, Sharyn Craig

Sew Much Fun: 14 Projects to Stitch & Embroider, Oklahoma Embroidery Supply & Design

Shadow Quilts, Patricia Magaret & Donna Slusser

Shadow Redwork™ with Alex Anderson: 24 Designs to Mix and Match, Alex Anderson

Show Me How to Machine Quilt: A Fun, No-Mark Approach, Kathy Sandbach

Skydyes: A Visual Guide to Fabric Painting, Mickey Lawler

Smashing Sets: Exciting Ways to Arrange Quilt Blocks, Margaret J. Miller

Snowflakes & Quilts, Paula Nadelstern

Soft-Edge Piecing: Add the Elegance of Appliqué to Traditional-Style Patchwork Design, Jinny Beyer

Special Delivery Quilts, Patrick Lose

Start Quilting with Alex Anderson, 2nd Edition: Six Projects for First-Time Quilters, Alex Anderson

Stitch 'n Flip Quilts : 14 Fantastic Projects, Valori Wells

Stripes In Quilts, Mary Mashuta

Strips 'n Curves: A New Spin on Strip Piecing, Louisa L. Smith

Thimbleberries Housewarming, A: 22 Projects for Quilters, Lynette Jensen

Trapunto by Machine, Hari Walner

Travels with Peaky and Spike: Doreen Speckmann's Quilting Adventures, Doreen Speckmann

Visual Dance, The: Creating Spectacular Quilts, Joen Wolfrom

Wild Birds: Designs for Appliqué & Quilting, Carol Armstrong

Wildflowers: Designs for Appliqué and Quilting, Carol Armstrong

Workshop with Velda Newman, A: Adding Dimension to Your Quilts, Velda E. Newman

For more information write for a free catalog:
C&T Publishing, Inc.
P.O. Box 1456
Lafayette, CA 94549
(800) 284-1114
http://www.ctpub.com
e-mail: ctinfo@ctpub.com

For quilting supplies:
Cotton Patch Mail Order
3405 Hall Lane, Dept. CTB
Lafayette, CA 94549
e-mail: quiltusa@yahoo.com
web: www.quiltusa.com
(800) 835-4418 • (925) 283-7883

Note: Fabrics used in the quilts shown may not be currently available since fabric manufacturers keep most fabrics in print for only a short time.